D0065605

THE
FAITH
THAT
Works

By
Peter Youngren

Graceworld Resources
PO Box 2108, Vista, CA 92085 USA
190 Railside Rd, Toronto, ON M3A 1A3 Canada

ISBN 978-1-987948-00-4

This book is dedicated to my best friend, my beloved wife, Taina; my partner, confidant and constant companion.

Thank you, Taina, for your genuine spirituality, your faith and your constant encouragement.

I love you dearly.

TABLE OF CONTENTS

Introduction

My dad was a diabetic. The sickness affected everything about our life. Mealtimes were exact; 8 AM, noon and 5 PM, and even the slightest variance of timing would increase the chance that my dad would go into an insulin coma. The whole family was on the lookout for signs that the insulin and sugar levels may be out of balance, but as I was the oldest child, my mother depended especially on me.

Sometimes my dad became unconscious unexpectedly. One Saturday morning, when I was 9 or 10 years old, my dad and I were shopping on a busy street in a nearby town. It was about 10:30 in the morning. This was considered a "safe time," when an insulin coma was unlikely to occur, half way between breakfast and lunch. The picture is still clear in my mind. Dad suddenly stopped on the sidewalk and appeared oblivious to his surroundings. I called out, "Dad," but he didn't react. After a few moments, he slumped to the ground and went into a coma. I remember the rush of adrenaline and desperation, as I ran from store to store trying to find orange juice or something with lots of sugar that I could give to Dad, to try to get him out of the coma, all the while shouting to get people to call an ambulance.

I learned to dislike sickness. It wreaks havoc in people's lives. Sometimes I've heard well-intentioned Christians suggest that God wants to put sickness on someone, in order to teach them a lesson of holiness or dependence on the Lord. It always struck me as cruel. I can't imagine anyone who has experienced sickness and pain up close to feel that way.

My father was a deeply devout Christian, but as far back as I can remember, he was struggling to have faith to be healed. He wanted so much for this power, called faith, to be present in his life. Being a Bible believer, he knew that faith makes everything possible. Yet, that faith seemed elusive.

At the age of 15, I traveled with my dad to Chicago, Illinois, to attend a convention where the famous Kathryn Kuhlman, renowned for healings and miracles, was one of the featured speakers. Dad wanted to go to a place where there was more faith. I was deeply touched by Kathryn Kuhlman's service and her reliance on the Holy Spirit. Still the healing that my dad longed for eluded him. We returned to my home country of Sweden, enriched by what we had experienced in the United States, but still no healing.

It was about this time in my life that I began to devour books about healing and faith. I wanted so much to have the same faith as those early disciples in the Book of Acts. It seemed that I could see faith in others, but what about me?

Three years after the visit to Chicago, I enrolled in Bible College in Providence, Rhode Island, and a year later I was invited to conduct 15 days of Gospel meetings in Toronto. A local pastor had rented a 1000-seat tent, and I was the featured speaker. Every night I preached under a canopy with a big banner strung from pole to pole announcing, "Teenage evangelist from Sweden." It was an exciting time. I had never prayed publicly for God to heal sick people. Maybe it was just youthful enthusiasm, but I went ahead the very first night and said a prayer for the sick. I sent everybody home without asking if anybody had been healed. To my amazement two days later a man approached me, claiming that for the last four years his right ear had been completely deaf, and that it had opened when I prayed. His wife standing beside him nodded, adding that she would always have to speak to him from his left side, or else she would have to shout really loudly.

I was thrilled. This was the first time that I had received a testimony of healing. I still didn't think I had much faith, but obviously something was working.

After the Toronto meeting, I began holding "revivals" in churches. Sometimes these meetings would be extended to four, five or even six weeks. A few years l was busy conducting international Gospel Campaigns, in stadiums and on large open fields, where tens of thousands, sometimes hundreds of thousands would congregate at one time. First and foremost in each meeting was to invite people to receive Christ as Savior. Then I would invariably pray for the sick and ask those who were healed to give witness to what had happened. Miracles and healings were frequent, but still it seemed like faith and unbelief were always present simultaneously, battling for dominance in my mind. In spite of my intense desire to have mountain-moving faith, there was a constant sense of not quite measuring up. Still, God was greater than my struggles and confirmed my preaching of Jesus Christ with miracles that would demonstrate to those present that Christ is alive.

The search for ever-increasing faith continued.

My struggle ended the day I recognized my own total inability to produce faith. I understood that all the healings I had seen were not the result of any great spiritual performance or achievement that I had accomplished. In fact, as I reviewed the hundreds of healings I had witnessed, it seemed like the greatest miracle had happened when I felt the weakest.

I discovered that the only faith that works is the faith of Jesus Christ. He believes, when the limitations of my mind say that it is impossible. The only sensible response was to consider myself dead from my own ability to produce faith, and yield to Christ's own faith resident in me. His faith now became my faith. The faith that created everything, the limitless faith of God, was available to be expressed through a limited human being. God had made His faith available to me.

This book is an invitation to explore this faith. It empowers you to speak to mountains and they will move. And you don't need a warehouse of this kind of faith; it only takes a mustard seed.

My dad is with Christ now. I think of him often. The religious environment that he was familiar with was one where faith was something that we had to produce. I'm glad for everything my dad taught me. Seeing his sickness up close set me on a journey to discover faith.

In 2005, after more than a quarter of a century of healing ministry, standing in the national Stadium of Guyana, South America, I said something I've never said before. Up to that point, all I had ever told people was to have more faith, to believe God more, and God had helped me to see many people healed and blessed. As I looked at people from one end of the stadium to another—among those present were blind, deaf, cancer patients and some who were obviously deformed—these words came out of my mouth:

Everything in me wants to believe that you will leave this stadium healed, and I know that you also want to believe that Christ heals or you'd probably not be here. Yet, my faith is weak, because while I believe, I also have doubts. I wonder what if nothing happens and maybe you are thinking the same. So instead of trying to have faith, I declare that I am dead to my ability to produce the faith that moves mountains. But, I'm alive to the faith of Jesus Christ. Somebody here tonight believes, and that somebody is Jesus Christ. I will not pray for you with my feeble attempt to have faith, but with the faith of the Son of God.

From that moment, faith has never been the same to me. Faith—mountain moving faith—is produced by Christ in us. It's the faith that works. And it is readily available for everyone.

ONE

The Faith Dilemma

The nineteen-year-old preacher was crouched on a rock just behind the little country church. Desperate to remain unnoticed by the people entering through the front door he agonized, "Oh God, give me faith. I'm trying so hard to believe. How can I have the faith of those early disciples?" He was clenching his fists in turmoil until his knuckles began to turn white, sincerely pleading with God. That young preacher was me.

Oh, how I wanted to experience God's power just as I saw it in the Book of Acts. The healing ministry of Jesus intrigued me. I wanted to see miracles, but I knew from Scripture that I needed faith. Without faith it is impossible to please God, and I sure wanted my life to be pleasing to the Lord.

Many people feel they have some faith, but not enough. They wonder: "How can my faith grow large enough, so that I can receive from the Lord?" It is as if you were dangling a succulent bone in front of a dog, but you never let him put his teeth into it. Sincere Christians know that they need faith, and they seek for it, but it seems so elusive. In spite of sincere attempts to produce faith, many find themselves coming up short. At times this can feel like an endless treadmill to nowhere. To chase after faith as if it were a divine empowering to be caught only by those who try hard enough is tiresome, frustrating and often leads to complete resignation; "faith just doesn't work for me."

Others experience anguish over their perceived lack of faith, especially those who are in a desperate need, and who may feel that a miracle has eluded them due to their lack of faith. Often this leads to self-condemning thoughts: "What's wrong with me? Why can't I have faith like others have?"

This book is an invitation to a discovery. We will look at what faith is, what makes it work, and how you can enjoy the same faith that Jesus demonstrated. We will look at two people, the only two, to whom Jesus ascribed not only faith, but "great faith." By the time you finish the pages of this book you will rejoice because you will know that you too can enjoy this "great faith."

Everyone who has received Jesus Christ as Savior already has faith; we only need to know how to work with what we have. God has dealt the measure of faith to every person (Roman 12:3). Just like a car must have an engine or it cannot be truly called the car, a believer has faith; otherwise he is not a believer. The moment we respond to God's love through Jesus, He imparts faith to us. You will discover how the faith you already have will increase and flourish; it will be made easy.

Faith will flow through you as freely as the blood flows through your veins.

This "real faith" will not depend on your performance, but instead it is fully wrapped up in Jesus. Once you experience this kind of faith, a new world of possibilities will open to you.

One of the two to whom Jesus ascribed great faith was a mother crying out for her child, and the other was a Roman military officer desperately looking for healing on behalf of a paralyzed servant. Who were these two? What were their secrets? What is "great faith?" How can we enjoy this kind of faith today?

Both of these individuals encountered Jesus before He died and rose again. They were still in the time period that the Bible refers to as the Old Covenant. Their stories are included in the Scriptures for our benefit. The principles of faith that were applicable to these two are examples for us who live in the New Covenant—the time period after Jesus died and rose again. The only difference between them and us is that we live in the "it is finished" time of history. As we will see in chapter 3, the gift of faith that they enjoyed is now readily available to everyone.

Faith is the key to everything God has promised us. Jesus stated that even the smallest measurement of faith, a grain of mustard seed, is enough to speak to a mountain of impossibilities and it will be moved. Consequently, to have faith is a key to God's unlimited blessings. We certainly want to know what faith, the real faith, is, but more importantly, *how* do we get it?

The answers may surprise you. In fact, the two individuals Jesus referred to as having "great faith" didn't even seem to know that they had any faith at all. Furthermore, they were not looking for faith, or even aware that they were supposed to have it. Neither one of them suggested that they had faith or lack of faith. They seemed to have no concern about attaining faith, it was not on the radar screen of their mind. Still, Jesus said they had it.

This tells us that faith may be different than what we have been taught to expect. After all, how is it possible that those who struggle and search for faith don't have it, while others have faith, even great faith, though they are unaware that they need it?

Here is the dilemma for many. On the one hand, believers acknowledge that God is the source of everything. Everything we need is already available from God. If we need healing, joy, prosperity, blessings or miracles, God has all of these for us and the Bible gives us numerous promises about God's willingness to give to us. Jesus said, "Ask, and you shall receive." James writes, "You have not because you ask not." Jesus stated that God's willingness to give far exceeds that of a parent desiring to give good things to their children. "If you then, being evil, know how to give good gifts to your children, how much more will your heavenly Father *give* the Holy Spirit to those who ask Him!" (Luke 11:13).

If God has what we need, and if He is willing to give

to us, then why is it that some find it very difficult to receive anything from the Lord? This is a valid question. Often the answer given is, "God is not the problem: we are." At a glance this statement seems reasonable, but before accepting it as truth, let's examine further.

First, God has never changed. Jesus is the same yesterday, today and forever. When we read of Jesus' ministry, He never refused healing or blessing to anyone who came to Him. Jesus was never the problem. So far, so good!

Are we then the problem? In the only instance in Jesus' earthly ministry, where a group of people did not receive a blessing, the reason given is unbelief. I'm referring to the case of the people in Jesus' hometown of Nazareth. Scripture is clear that Jesus "marveled" at their unbelief and He could not do any mighty miracle there. It's a clear-cut case, Jesus was not the problem; the people of Nazareth were.

Before we jump to conclusions, we need to also ask, "Other than the people of Nazareth and their obvious rejection of Jesus Christ, in what way could we be a problem, since all we want is to receive from God, and He is willing to give to us?" Here is where we easily get caught in a trap of self-loathing and condemnation, which is never from God. Jesus stated unequivocally that He did not come to condemn people (John 3:17). The book of Hebrews clearly tells us that Christ's finished work is to free us from sin consciousness (Hebrews 10:2), so an introspective self-analysis of your supposed faults and failures is not helpful.

The trap is that we may erroneously conclude that the reason that we have not yet received from God is to be found by looking within ourselves, searching our hearts, to see what hindrances to faith may be in us. Though this may sound holy and religious, it is the opposite. It is destructive. Introspection will not produce positive results or bring God's blessing into our lives. On the contrary, to look inwardly will only lead to disappointment and insecurity.

To look at our self and how well we have performed our religious duties is called "dead works." a phrase found several times in the Book of Hebrews. We are called to turn from dead works. The remedy for unbelief is not in introspective condemnation, but in looking at what Christ has accomplished for us. This serves to "purge your conscience from dead works to serve the living God" (Hebrews 9:14). Faith and religious "works" are opposites. That's why real faith does not operate well in an environment that is focused on religious works.

Our perception changes in the light of what Jesus Christ has done on our behalf. Good things happen when our eyes are open to Christ's finished work. The problem of the people of Nazareth was simply that they did not view Jesus properly. If they had only recognized Him for who He is, they could have received the same healing, blessing and miracles that people in other towns enjoyed.

Many determine that the reason they have not yet received from God is lack of faith. They question how they can acquire more faith. This idea that you lack faith is reinforced by people who remind you that "you need more faith." This statement is often followed by a suggestion of how to obtain this elusive quality called faith; study the principles of faith, read the Bible more, make positive confessions of God's promises, visualize positive results, rebuke the devil, and so on. These are certainly valuable spiritual activities, but when the answers to their prayers still elude earnest believers, they are told, "You still need more faith," and so their struggle continues.

Some work very hard at controlling what they say so as not to speak anything negative. Others put Scripture verses on prominent display in their home and car to always remind them of what God has said. This is good. I also display Scripture verses and statements by Jesus to keep them ever before me. However sadly, some do everything that they can possibly think of and still it seems nothing happens. Faith appears increasingly to be a mystery. "How can I have more faith?" becomes the nagging question without any real answers.

If you pay attention to the words of Jesus, you notice how important faith is. Jesus rebuked the disciples for their lack of faith with words like, "Oh ye of little faith," or "Why do you have no faith?" The only time you see Jesus slightly irritated with the disciples is when He notices a lack of faith. So much more reason for us to pursue faith, since we certainly do not want to frustrate Jesus.

To some the struggle for faith is compounded by the words in the Book of Hebrews, "But without faith it is impossible to please Him, for he who comes to God must believe that He is, and that He is a rewarder of those who diligently seek Him" (Hebrews 11:6). Again, we are faced with the crucial necessity of faith. Sincere Christians don't want to displease God, so once again many conclude that we must try harder to have faith. You'll notice that I refer to "believers" and "sincere Christians," because I realize that it is highly unlikely that anyone who is not sincere in their faith would even bother to read this book. That's the point—sincere believers struggle for faith, all the while feeling that they have come up short, that they are not good enough. Surely, God must have a better way.

Some may have encountered what I call the "faith police." These are individuals who think they have great faith and like to point out lack of faith in others. They seem to have all the answers for others: "You were not healed because you need more faith," is their explanation. These individuals are often well-intentioned, but their words still condemn others for not thinking, confessing or imagining the promises of God as they should. The problem is further compounded because many of these who I call the "faith police" do not themselves enjoy the blessings of God. In fact, some of them are grumpy and condemning of others. When they themselves face impossible circumstances, they also become discouraged and find themselves unable to obtain the answer to their prayers.

Do you see the perpetual problem we encounter on this treadmill of the pursuit of faith? The more we try to have faith, the more it seems we never quite have it. It seems as elusive as the rainbow. You see the rainbow in the sky with its beautiful colors and majestic arch; yet as you race toward it, it vanishes out of sight. Some have given up on faith altogether. You can hear them sigh, "Faith is not for me. It works for others, but I can't get it to work in my life."

Jesus said, "Assuredly, I say to you, if you have faith as a mustard seed, you will say to this mountain, 'Move from here to there,' and it will move; and nothing will be impossible for you" (Matthew 17:20).

There is no ambiguity in Jesus' words. Faith in the mere size of a mustard seed will enable you to speak to a mountain to move, and it will move. We must take Jesus' words at face value. There are only two possible explanations of His statement. Either Jesus was telling the truth or He wasn't. Again, since you are reading this book, I assume that you believe that Jesus is the Truth. What then are we to make of the fact that many people claim to have faith, but their "mountain" has not moved? Could it be that what we may have called "faith" is not the kind of faith Jesus spoke of at all? Consider this:

The God-kind of faith, mountain-moving faith, is completely different from mental believing.

The contrast is like night and day. Mental believing is exercised by almost every person on a daily basis. Our whole system of society, whether banking, postal service, or business is built on mental believing. When we open a box of cereal, we do not logically and scientifically scrutinize every fiber or every flake; we believe what the package claims about the content. When we drop an envelope in the mailbox, we believe it will be delivered. With little exception, and unless we hear something different on the radio, television, or read it in a newspaper, we believe in these functions of society. This kind of believing has to do with the mind. It is metaphysical. It has to do with reason, logic and mental comprehension. As beneficial as mental believing is in order for us to function in society, it is not the kind of "faith" Jesus spoke of when He referred to faith as a grain of mustard seed, the kind which enables you to speak to a mountain and it will move.

Jesus didn't say that if you have faith as a grain of mustard seed, you will *at times* be able to move mountains. No, Jesus made a blanket statement that "Nothing will be impossible for you," and the mountain "will move." This seems totally unrealistic and illogical to natural thinking. After repeated attempts at this kind of faith, some shrug it off, "It doesn't work for me."

In many churches today if the pastor were to announce a series of teachings on faith, there would be little excitement. The reason is that people have already heard numerous teachings on faith and feel disillusioned when it has not worked as they were told it would.

I have seen thousands of people healed: the lame, blind, deaf, mute, lepers, cancer cases, humanly impossible cases. I have walked away from many Gospel services with shouts of rejoicing echoing in my ears as people celebrated what Christ had done for them. I rejoiced with them, but in my mind's eye I could also vividly see those who had not been healed. My heart ached for them. I have seen the lame walk, but I have also witnessed scenes where concerned Christians gathered around a wheelchair encouraging the sick person, rebuking the devil, even lifting the suffering one out of the wheelchair and trying to get him to walk only to have to put him back in the chair.

This is a far cry from Jesus, who said that faith in the smallest measurement, like a grain of mustard seed, means that "nothing will be impossible."

I don't claim to know everything, but the truths I share in this book are answers to questions I have had. Is there a faith that works? What is a real faith? My own soul has been satisfied by the answers I bring to you. Jesus has ministered these truths to me and faith has become easy. I don't struggle for faith, because the more I struggle the less real faith I have. There's a whole other way. The moment we cease our pursuit of faith and allow the ability of Jesus to flow through us, something remarkable happens. All things are possible when Jesus' own faith becomes our faith.

"I live by the faith *of* the Son of God" (Galatians 2:20), is how Paul, the apostle, said it.

Unfortunately, some translations render this verse, faith in the son of God, not faith of the Son of God. There is a huge difference between faith in Christ and the faith *of* Christ. While faith in God is wonderful, this term can be misconstrued into a religious self-effort. When some hear of faith in God, they go back on that old treadmill of dead works, which only leads to more complaining and wondering why they don't have enough faith. Gratefully the King James Version of the Bible translates this verse in the only way that makes sense in the context:

The faith of the Son of God.

The apostle is not describing his attempt to have faith in Christ, but he is declaring that the very faith of Christ has become his. My faith is the faith of Christ working through me. That's the topic of this book. We are not exploring more hoops that we must jump through in order to have faith; we are 100% focused on the only faith that works—the faith of Jesus Christ.

Simon Peter gives a corroborating testimony when he explains how the man, who had been lame from birth, was healed, not by Simon Peter's faith or holiness, but by the faith that works through Jesus (Acts 3:16).

Maybe you, my reader, have struggled and wondered what could be the obstacle in your life. Possibly you have been encouraged to look inwardly to discover and root out hindrances. A lady recently approached me, saying, "Peter, I am concerned that there are hindrances in me and that's why my family is not enjoying healing." I responded gently to her, "Surely there are hindrances in you, and furthermore there are hindrances in me and in every person who ever sought for God's blessing. If the truth were told, we could find hindrances in every person if we look hard enough. However, we are not to research or try to discern the hindrances within us, because it would be an endless and fruitless pursuit. The more we look at ourselves and others, the more we will invent reasons that explain to our mind why we should not experience the blessings of God."

I continued my response to the woman, "Don't look for hindrances in you, because you'll find too many to ever deal with, but rather look at Jesus in whom there are no hindrances." I tried to help her by pointing her to the Scripture which says that all the promises of God are ours in Christ Jesus, not on the basis of what we have done, but because of Him.

Paul, the apostle, said it this way, "For the Son of God, Jesus Christ, who was preached among you...was not Yes and No, but in Him was Yes. For all the promises of God in Him are Yes, and in Him Amen, to the glory of God through us" (2 Corinthians 1:19-20).

Notice that God's promises are "yes" and "amen" in Jesus. This way God gets all the glory as He works through us.

There's a human propensity towards religious legalism that blinds our eyes from seeing the obvious. Often this Scripture has been taught, as if it said that the promises of God are "yes" in Jesus Christ and that we had to add our "amen" to it. That would make the fulfillment of God's promises a joint effort. A plain reading tells us that both the "yes" and the "amen" are in Jesus Christ. He has accomplished it all and our part is simply to receive.

Don't construe my words to mean that we should not obey God, or that it doesn't matter how we behave or act. On the contrary, when we discover that the promises of God are already ours in Jesus, we will want to be even more obedient to Christ and His finished work.

In the Old Testament, before the death and resurrection of Jesus, people tried to obey God <u>in order to obtain</u> His promises. We, who live in the New Covenant, after the death and resurrection of Jesus, also obey God, but our motivation is different. We are obedient **because God's promises are already ours**.

It's a world of difference between trying to get something and knowing that you already have it. If we already know that God's favor has been given to us, it makes no sense to try to obtain it. At the time of writing this, Taina and I have guests in our home. We have told them to help themselves to whatever they need, that whatever is in our house is theirs. It would be frustrating every time they wanted a glass of water, a cup coffee, or a piece of bread, if they came asking for it.

What's been given is given. Similarly, we don't seek for God's favor; it is already given in and through Jesus Christ.

In the Old Testament people made sacrifices and said prayers in order to obtain blessings from God, while now in the New Testament we do good works <u>because of</u> all Christ has done for us. They were obedient to God in order to please Him; we are obedient to God because He has saved us and given us a new life. God is now pleased because of what Jesus has done.

Before Jesus' death and resurrection, people petitioned God for His blessings. This kind of prayer is no longer appropriate in light of Jesus' finished work. The apostle Paul wrote, "Blessed be the God and Father of our Lord Jesus Christ, who <u>has blessed us</u> with every spiritual blessing in the heavenly places in Christ" (Ephesians 1:3). "Blessed" is past tense. We don't need to ask for that which we already have. This is an eye-opener to many. Some may wonder how we pray if all things are already given to us. Instead of petitioning God, we thank God for the blessings we have in Christ.

We also ask the Holy Spirit to open our eyes to see what we have *now*. That's how Paul, the apostle, prayed for the Ephesian believers, "The eyes of your understanding being enlightened; that you may know what is the hope of His calling, what are the riches of the glory of His inheritance in the saints, and what is the exceeding greatness of His power toward us who believe, according to the working of His mighty power" (Ephesians 1:18-19).

Do you see the stark difference? We do not pray in order to get blessed, but we pray asking God to show us more clearly the inheritance we already have.

Today, it is very common for Christians to act as if they didn't have anything. You can hear it in prayers: "Oh Lord, give me your power; come and bless us; send your anointing"; etc. While these statements may make the petitioner appear to be humble and dependent on the Lord, these prayers actually fly in the face of what Jesus has done. All power, blessing and anointing have already been transferred to our account.

In order to have great faith it is important to recognize on which side of the cross we live. We live after the cross; Jesus has already put away the world's sins and carried our sicknesses. This is vastly different from life prior to Christ's death and resurrection. Christ's righteousness has now been credited to our account, and on the basis of His righteousness we inherit all of God's goodness and promises.

We no longer love in order to obtain God's love; we love God because He first loved us. We pray *not* to obtain the victory or the blessing, but because the victory is already ours. Similarly, we don't try to have faith by our own effort. Instead:

We have faith, because we are linked with the author and the finisher of faith—Jesus Christ.

In chapter 4, we will begin our careful exploration of the two individuals who enjoyed "great faith." We will look at how they connected with Jesus and saw their "mountains" move. How did they tap into this Jesus-kind of faith? What was their secret?

But I caution you, don't jump ahead. In chapters 2 and 3, I will build a foundation for the faith of Jesus Christ to operate in you. You're about to become deeply rooted in the faith of Jesus Christ. Even the best teaching will be ineffective without the Holy Spirit. My prayer for you is that the Holy Spirit will reveal Jesus, the source of faith in you.

TWO

Faith Works by Love

J ust as there is no smoke without fire, there is no faith without love, because "faith works by love" (Galatians 5:6). No
matter how hard we try to have faith, it will never happen
without personal knowledge of Christ's love, a knowledge
that goes beyond academic understanding.

If you're fortunate enough to have experienced love from
another person, you are indeed blessed. Think of the highest
form of love you've ever known, maybe the love of a parent,
a spouse, or a mentor. Think of how that person expressed
love towards you. Maybe you would say that they <u>had</u> love
for you. Still there's a vast difference between *having* love
and *being* love.

God is love (1 John 4:8).

People can have love; God *has* love and God *is* love. If God only has love, there is the possibility that the love supply will be reduced, due to circumstances. However, if God is love, then anything we know of God must be congruent with who He is. God will never act contrary to His nature. If God is love, anything God does will be consistent with love.

Love loves!

If God is love and suddenly stopped loving you, He would no longer be God.

One man angrily warned me, "Don't go overboard on God's love, because after all love is only one of God's characteristics." Students of theology may list God's attributes: righteousness, peace, mercy, justice, etc., and will often add, "Of course, love is the number one characteristic of God." However, this misses the point.

God's nature and God's attributes are not one and the same. God's nature represents who God is, the essence of God, while His attributes are the result of who He is. Righteousness, justice, peace and every other attribute of God are byproducts of His nature—Love. His attributes can never be in conflict with His nature. To warn against an overemphasis of God's love is the same as warning against God. Look at this Scripture:

> But God is rich in mercy towards us **because** of his great love, wherewith he loved us. (Ephesians 2:4)

Mercy, which is the Hebrew word *hesed*, means loving kindness. This is a characteristic of God, but notice that it exists only "because of his great love." This is true of every attribute of God. Even God's anger flows from His love, as God is angry with the terrible things that sin is doing to destroy people's lives.

Faith is no exception; it is also a byproduct of love. Love makes faith possible.

It should not be surprising that the devil has done an extraordinary job of distorting the meaning of God's love. If we don't know what God's love is, we can never have the faith that works, because the two are inter-connected.

Any lie about God must be a lie about love, because God is love.

If people have a twisted image of God, they have a twisted image of love. Sadly, there is an ugly religious version of love masquerading as God. We call it love, but it really isn't. Instead, it is a hideous distortion that reduces God's love into mere human love, and robs us of the gift of faith.

I realize that there's a risk that you, the reader, will skip ahead to the next chapter at this point. After all the topic of love is so common that we automatically think we already know everything about it. I caution you to go slowly at this point. I'm about to use certain terminologies that you may be familiar with, but pay close attention, as you may see these in a different light than ever before.

There are three words in the Greek New Testament that are translated "love" in our Bible:

Phileo means brotherly love, affection and fondness.

Agape is the God-kind of love. The word was rarely used in the Greek language prior to the writing of the New

Testament. It had to be redefined in order to describe this new kind of love, a love that had been forgotten for millenniums, until Jesus reintroduced it.

Eros was the most common word for love in the Greek culture, much like we use love in our culture; "I love this pizza," " I love my dog," "I love my spouse" and "I love shopping."

Eros is the love of the lovely, the beautiful and the desirable. It is rooted in the object of the desire. Eros is awakened by the beauty of the beloved. Before you married your spouse, you saw something lovely, beautiful and desirable. Soon you told your friends that you were "in love."

Keep in mind that these three types of love are all from God. God invented "Eros" and "Phileo" for us to enjoy. Eros gave us the arts, architecture, beautiful sculptures and the love between a man and a woman. Still, Eros is never used to describe God's love.

To distinguish between Eros and Agape in relationship to God is crucial. Eros is incapable of loving the ugly, the disharmonious. It is repulsed by anything it considers substandard. The problem with Eros is that it is changeable and unreliable. All human love must be earned and maintained. Even the most beautiful love relationship can disintegrate when one of the parties becomes abusive and destructive.

The source of Eros is **the object**—the beloved. The source of Agape is **the giver** of love—God.

If the object of the love becomes less lovely, then Eros is on shaky ground. Agape can never be altered because it is not moved by the object. God is Agape and Agape is God, and God can never be shaken.

God's love for you is forever settled.

When religion talks about God's love, it is often described as a conditional love. Sadly, the great majority of humans look at God's love as Eros, or maybe Super-Eros, a kind of superhuman love, but a love that is still conditional.

Of course, students of the Bible, and maybe you the reader, already knew that Agape is the Greek word to describe God's love. However, it is one thing to know linguistically that God is Agape, and quite another to know the difference between God's love and human love.

Many think that God is looking for something desirable in us in order to release His love and blessing. That is the characteristic of Eros. If God's love is conditional, we will forever be in doubt; are we pleasing enough to God, are we good and holy enough?

When I look at Peter Youngren, what do I see? Do I see a person who is good enough for God's love? Put yourself in the picture. Do you see yourself as a little bit less than what you think you should be? Are you a good enough wife? Husband? Parent? Church member? Worshiper?

The deception of religion is that God loves the highest, the best and the most desirable. This breeds the idea that in order to receive God's love, you must be passionate enough, show enough righteousness, be holy enough, and have enough faith. Only then will you be included in God's circle. You hear statements like, "If you want God's best, you have to give your best." Others talk about becoming a "God chaser," as if God were hard to get a hold of and difficult to find. It's the old illustration of a ladder going up to heaven, where we try with every religious work to climb ever higher to get closer to God. You may think, well what's wrong with that? Isn't it good if people are chasing after God? Should we not tell people to sacrifice for God? Be more fervent in service to God?

The Book of Proverbs tells us that "there is a way that seems right" to a person, but "the end thereof is death" (Proverbs 16:25). What seems so holy, good and "right" can in the end be destructive. A distorted view of that makes God out to be a deity who only blesses us if we show ourselves desirable and worthy.

The truth in the face of religious deception is that God loves you at your worst, in your darkest hour, when you are at your worst or your best, in failure or success. Absolutely nothing can separate you from the love of God in Christ Jesus (Romans 8:38).

Faith does not work through the Eros kind of love. As long as we think that God blesses us on the basis of something desirable in us, we can never have the faith that works. The thought that God loves us only when there is something beautiful in us is incompatible with real faith. Real faith flourishes when we discover God's unconditional love. Every obstacle is removed by knowing His love.

Faith works with Agape. This love of God is an unconditional, reckless, almost insane kind of love. It is the love exhibited in Luke chapter 15, where the father in the story threw caution to the wind and ran towards the prodigal son, who had wasted the family's fortune. The father was disinterested in what the son could do for him. There was no secret agenda, only unconditional love.

Adam knew the Agape love of God in the garden, but he

walked away from it. Over the centuries Agape was forgotten. Even the greatest of the prophets only saw a glimpse of God's love and often didn't understand what they saw. Even Isaiah, the evangelist of the Old Testament, couldn't wrap his mind around what he saw of God's love, and had to settle for words like, "eye has not seen, nor has ear heard, nor has it entered into the heart of man what God has prepared for those who love him." It would take another 700 years after the prophet Isaiah before Agape was reintroduced. When Paul, the apostle, quoted Isaiah, he would add, "but God has revealed them to us by his Spirit." In other words, what Isaiah could not put into words, what was too much for him, we now know because of Jesus Christ.

Jesus reintroduced the real love of God.

Why did Jesus come?

The standard evangelical answer is that Jesus came to die for our sins. Of course, that is good as far as it goes, but it is hugely inadequate. Jesus came to reintroduce God's loving thoughts that had been lost after Adam chose to walk away from his Creator. Jesus said, "No one has seen God at any time; the only begotten Son, who is in the bosom of the father, he has declared him" (John 1:18).

Strong words! Jesus claims that He's the only one qualified to show us who God is. No wonder the religious leaders wanted to crucify Him. Religion has never accepted Agape—unconditional love. Ever since Adam walked away from God to create a god in his own image, the human understanding of God has been distorted. Adam rejected Agape, lost his sense of purpose and became driven to reinvent the meaning of life.

Two thousand years later, at a place called Golgotha, where Jesus was about to be crucified, the religious leaders shouted, "Away with him, we don't want this man." Religion has always wanted to do away with Agape, to put the real God out of business. Real faith can never exist as long as we accept the "god" of religion, which makes God's love conditional. We will always wonder if we have sufficiently met those conditions.

Faith works by Agape, unconditional love! If God's love remains unchanged in our darkest moment, then there is nothing that stands in our way from receiving everything that God has provided for us.

Agape is everlasting love. "Yes, I have loved you with an everlasting love; therefore with loving kindness I have drawn you" (Jeremiah 31:3). This love has no beginning, no end. It is outside of time and space. It unilaterally loves you and loves its enemies and keeps seeking and drawing until the lost is found.

Agape is personal. The apostle wrote, "I live by the faith of the Son of God, who loved me and gave himself for **me**" (Galatians 2:20). This goes beyond God's love for the world, it's profoundly personal; He loves me and gave Himself for me.

Agape is scandalous love. The Bible reports God's love for the five-time divorcee, known as the Samaritan woman, who became an evangelist. The man who wrote almost a third of the New Testament "breathed murder" towards Christians. Jesus ate and drank with notorious sinners and professional swindlers known as tax collectors, which was scandalous to the religious leaders.

But we don't have to look any further than in our own mirror. If every thought, act, envy and sin was known about any one of us, we would have to admit that God's grace is scandalously generous towards us.

Agape love is freely given. The prophet Hosea spoke on behalf of God, "I heal their backsliding, I love them freely" (Hosea 14:4). God's love is without price.

Agape is only understood through Jesus Christ. John, who called himself "the disciple whom Jesus loved," wrote:

In this the love of God was manifested toward us, that God has sent his only begotten Son into the world, that we might live through him. And this is love, not that we love God, but that he loved us and sent his Son to be the propitiation for our sins. (1 John 4:8-10)

Sometimes it is hard for the Western mindset to understand how God's love can be wrapped up in one person, and that we are all identified with that person—Jesus Christ.

This idea that a family or a whole nation is "in" one person was common to the Middle Eastern mindset. Remember the story of David and Goliath. The Philistines agreed to see themselves in the giant Goliath, while Israel saw itself in David, the shepherd boy. Their mutual agreement was that if Goliath won the battle, then all the Philistines had won and Israel would serve them. Alternately, if David emerged victorious, then all of Israel was victorious. The idea was that what happened to one man—the official representative—happened to all.

Humanity's first official representative was Adam. When

he refused to continue in relationship with God and distanced himself from God's love plan, Adam's disobedience affected the human race. Generations were "lost" because of being disconnected from Agape.

Humanity needed a fresh start. Jesus—the last Adam—provided that restart. Since the relationship between God and people was broken through Adam, the instinctive longing for a restart had been there. Often people didn't know that it was God they were looking for, just that something was amiss.

The human craving for Agape goes as far back as a record of history. Possibly the oldest book of the Bible, the Book of Job, describes this quest. Job wrote about God: "For He is not a man, as I am, that I should answer Him, and we should come together in judgment. Neither is there any mediator between us, that He might lay his hand on both of us" (Job 9: 32-33).

Job's cry for a mediator is fulfilled by Jesus Christ, "For there is one mediator between God and man, the Man Christ Jesus" (1 Timothy 2:5). A mediator is a go-between, one who acts as a guarantor for both parties involved in a negotiation. In the covenant that Jesus Christ provided for us, God the Father guarantees the divine side and God the Son is the guarantor of the human side.

Jesus did not need a covenant with the Father. When He went to the cross, He did it *as* us and *for* us. Humanity, with all the evil that had been passed down through generations, was wrapped up in Jesus Christ.

An Italian artist created the famous *Ecce Homo* painting, which shows Pontius Pilate leaning over a balcony looking towards the crowd below, while pointing his one hand in a backward motion towards Jesus. The Latin words Ecce Homo mean *Behold the Man*, but they can also be translated, **Behold humankind**.

That is the gospel. When we look at Jesus we see humankind. The old humanity, contaminated by the death passed on from Adam, was put on Christ. We see all the shame and guilt and evil that is associated with our first representative, Adam. But wait, there is more. We see the new humankind when Jesus comes out of the tomb as the Conqueror over evil and death.

Just like Christ died as us and for us, He arose as us and for us, to be the firstborn of many, that in Him every person may receive new life and become a new creation.

That's Agape!

Many struggle because they feel that their faith is inadequate. They think if they only had more faith they would receive more from God. Could it be that this is putting the proverbial cart before the horse? Instead of looking for more faith, could it be that the key is to look at how much God loves you?

One man told me, "My faith doesn't work, I've tried everything... memorized scriptures... visualized my miracle... confessed my sins... and nothing works." I want to shout it as loud as I can—when you know how much God loves you, your faith will work!

Faith is not an effort on our part to have confidence or to act boldly. Faith totally relies on God's love that was proven at the cross. Faith trusts in what God's grace has already provided. When we realize God's love through Jesus Christ, the struggle for faith is over.

I have conducted more than 400 Gospel Campaigns around the world. I have seen thousands with tired, sick bodies, racked with pain, receive healing from God, but I have also seen countless numbers of people who didn't seem to receive anything.

Here is what I have discovered. Those who look at how much faith they have often receive nothing, while those who become conscious of God's lavish love receive easily.

Agape love is the highest form of love. It is the same love that the Father had for Jesus Christ. Jesus assured us of the quality of God's love: "that the world may know that You have sent Me, and have **loved them as You have loved Me**" (John 17:23).

Sometimes we may think that God loves us, but it must be a lesser kind of love than the love that the Father has for Jesus. After all Jesus is perfect and consequently God must have more love for Jesus. No, Jesus assures us that the same quality of love He received from His heavenly father is the love that we receive from God.

The Scripture assures that, "Nothing can separate us from the love of God that is in Christ Jesus" (Romans 8:38). Your sins, failures, successes or shortcomings cannot change one absolute fact—you are loved by God.

Remember when Jesus told His disciples to go to the other side of the lake. Just looking at the other side, far away, would not get them there. They needed a boat to take them across the lake.

Many reach for healings, miracles, blessings and breakthroughs as if they were off in the distance "on the other side." What we really need is a boat to take us to that "other side." That boat is God's love!

When the prodigal son returned home, he offered himself for employment. He wanted to try to make things right by his own effort. He thought his father wanted to get paid back what he was owed. Little did he realize that all his father wanted was for the love and the relationship between the two of them to be restored. Only when he was deluged with his father's hugs and kisses did the son see how much he was loved. That's why I say that God has "hugs and kisses for you." Every miracle, every blessing is a kiss from God, who wants you to know how much you are loved.

Do you want more faith?

Don't try to get more faith. Instead, look at God's love. It is like a diamond with many facets. When you think you've seen it all, look again and realize that you just discovered another aspect of this limitless love.

THREE

Faith is Finished

Faith cannot be known apart from its source. The origin of faith is captured in the words, "Looking unto Jesus, the author and finisher of *our* faith" (Hebrews 12:2).

Author means originator, the beginning, the source.

Finisher means completer, no further work is needed, everything is already accomplished.

Jesus claims both these titles. Familiarity with biblical teaching may cause us to feel so accustomed to certain expressions that we don't stop and think about the real meaning. "Author and finisher" of faith is an amazing claim that faith has already been originated, and anything that has to do with faith has already been accomplished.

When a Scripture verse sounds very astounding, there can be a tendency for the translators to add one or two words that reduce the impact, and make it appear more reasonable. I'm not suggesting that this is done to purposely distort the meaning. Sometimes in the English language, or any other language, words need to be added in order to have a flow in the language. One of the advantages with the King James or the New King James version of the Bible is that when the translators add a word in order to get a better flow in the English language, that word or those words are in italics. When you look at the Scripture verse at the beginning of this chapter, you will notice that the word "our" is in italics.

The addition of the word *our* could serve to reduce the impact of the statement. Maybe someone believes God to answer a prayer and this verse could then be interpreted to mean that Christ has put the faith in my heart to pray and Christ will finish or make my faith better as I go along. Certainly, Christ helps us in our spiritual journey, but I suggest that there is something much bigger here. This goes far beyond a given situation, where we believe God to intervene in the situation. Look at the Scripture again, as we read it without the little word "our" added:

Looking unto Jesus, the author and finisher of faith.

The issue of faith itself has been settled. Faith is a completed fact. Faith is not something we struggle for; it is something we receive as a gift from God. If having faith depended on our effort, then Jesus obviously didn't fully become the author and finisher. If Jesus has done everything that is necessary for faith to function, there is nothing left for me to do but to receive that faith.

If this is true, how will this affect my life, my decisions

and my future? How will this alter the way that I approach God? The way I receive from God?

Before all those questions are answered, let's look at how and when Jesus authored faith, and how and when He finished faith. We know that a specific timeline can be determined. This faith came at a specific time.

> *The Scripture has confined all under sin, that the promise by faith in Jesus Christ might be given to those who believe. But* **before faith came***, we were kept under guard by the law, kept for the faith which would* **afterward** *be revealed. Therefore the law was our tutor to bring us to Christ, that we might be justified by faith. But* **after faith has come***, we are no longer under a tutor. For you are all sons of God through faith in Christ Jesus. (Galatians 3:22-26)*

Before and *after* are words that indicate a timeline. Faith came after the law was finished, or in the words of the epistle to the Romans, Jesus Christ is "the end of the law for righteousness to all those who believe" (Romans 10:4). All the requirements of the religious law, which could be held against us because we failed to live up to them, were nailed to the cross with Jesus Christ. His death fulfilled the law, made it obsolete, and opened the door to salvation by the faith of Christ.

Some have suggested that the law is still active, because Jesus said that He didn't come to destroy the law but to fulfill it. "Think not that I came to destroy the law, or the prophets: I'm not come to destroy, but to fulfill for verily I say unto you, that heaven and earth may pass, but one jot or one tittle shall in no wise pass from the law, <u>till all be fulfilled</u>" (Matthew 5:17-18).

I have noticed that when quoting the above reference, many don't finish the sentence. They cut it off before the little phrase, "till all be fulfilled." The gospel is that Jesus fulfilled all. Those who claim differently should put their money where their mouth is and get busy to keep all the law. If all is not fulfilled by Christ's finished work, we are still liable to keep not only the Ten Commandments, but every jot and tittle of the law. This includes every excruciating detail of ceremonial, religious and societal law. If our children are rebellious, we would have to stone them at the city gate, we would have to follow the dietary laws (forget shrimp, lobster, bacon or pork), laws for the monthly cycle of women, and hundreds of other instructions.

I'm not sure that even the most ardent proponent of the Mosaic law is willing to go that far. When it comes to the commandments, there's a tendency to cherry pick our favorite ones, while the Scripture is clear that if we are guilty in one area, we are guilty in all.

The Gospel is clear that Christ is the end of the law, and when the old system was finished, real faith—the faith of Christ—began. This new kind of faith is connected to the resurrection of Jesus Christ. "The word is near you, in your mouth and in your heart (that is, the word of faith which we preach): that if you confess with your mouth the Lord Jesus and believe in your heart **that God has raised Him from the dead**, you will be saved" (Romans 10:8-9).

Our faith is specifically tied to the resurrection of Jesus.

Obviously this wasn't possible before Jesus actually rose from the dead. Among those who lived before Jesus, Abraham came the closest to this new kind of faith, because he believed in the resurrection of his son Isaac, which was a type of the resurrection of Jesus. Famously, when Abraham brought his son Isaac to the top of Mount Moriah, he told his servants, "We'll be back." Abraham didn't expect to come back alone, but that even if he killed his son, God would raise him from the dead. That's why Abraham is an example of faith. "Therefore it is of faith that it might be according to grace, so that the promise might be sure to all … those who are of the faith of Abraham,… in the presence of Him whom he believed—God, who gives life to the dead and calls those things which do not exist as though they did" (Romans 4:16-18).

There you have it—Abraham believed that God gives life to the dead. The example of Abraham continues: "'it was accounted to him for righteousness.' Now it was not written for his sake alone that it was imputed to him, but also for us. It shall be imputed to us who believe in Him who raised up Jesus our Lord from the dead…" (Romans 4:22-24).

The faith era, foreshadowed by Abraham, originated or was "authored" by the resurrection of Jesus, but that's only half of the equation.

How was faith finished?

Again we go to the Book of Hebrews: "who being the brightness of His glory and the express image of His person, and upholding all things by the word of His power, when He had by Himself purged our sins, **sat down at the right hand of the Majesty on high**…" (Hebrews 1:3).

The Bible makes a lot out of the fact that Jesus sat down at the right hand of the Father in heaven. One writer calls it "the main point" (Hebrews 8:1). While we may sit down because we are tired, Jesus was never exhausted. He sat down because the work was finished. Everything needed for humanity's salvation was accomplished. All righteousness, forgiveness, healing, life and purpose that we would ever need was now available, and yes—even faith—had been provided.

Someone might ask, wasn't faith always here? Didn't God speak the universe into existence by faith? What about all the heroes of faith from the Old Testament? Yes, there were many manifestations of faith throughout history. Faith showed up from time to time in the lives of different people, but here's the difference. Faith was not readily available to everyone until Jesus Christ had finished His work.

This is truly good news. The faith of Jesus Christ is available to you right now. Stop striving to have faith, and instead receive the faith of Jesus. Maybe you pray like I often do out loud: "God, I thank you that I have the faith of Jesus Christ. My feeble attempt at faith is never sufficient, so I receive this faith that is a free gift."

This is a new concept to many, so to illustrate this truth, we look at a parallel area where the same principle is present. I'm talking about the Holy Spirit, who also manifested from time to time throughout history, but was only ever readily available to everyone after the Day of Pentecost. Jesus spoke of the Holy Spirit: "'He who believes in Me, as the Scripture has said, out of his heart will flow rivers of living water.' But this He spoke concerning the Spirit, whom those believing in

Him would receive; for **the Holy Spirit was not yet given,** because Jesus was not yet glorified" (John 7:38-39).

Jesus' message was clear, "the Holy Spirit was not yet given." How is that possible since the Holy Spirit showed up already in Genesis chapter 1 and "hovered over the waters"? Throughout the Old Testament writings there are many instances of when the Holy Spirit fell upon people. So what was Jesus talking about—the Holy Spirit was not yet given?

Again there's a timeline in the words that Jesus spoke. Jesus had to be glorified <u>before</u> the Holy Spirit would come to be readily available to everyone. Jesus' glorification happened when He sat down at the right hand of the Father, and from this exalted position He poured out the Holy Spirit. This changes everything:

The Holy Spirit is now readily available to everyone.

The God-kind of faith is now readily available to everyone.

In the first chapter of this book, I talked about people who struggle for more faith and yet never seem to have enough. When we discover that Jesus is the author and finisher of faith, our faith struggle is over. No more trying to have faith. The paradigm has shifted. We are no longer trying to imitate the Old Testament faith heroes—we simply look unto Jesus.

Notice, it doesn't say that we look for Jesus, as if He is far off in the distance. To "look unto" is to look like a baby would look at its mother after being well fed. To look unto one must be close up, like a baby clinging to his mother's breast.

What about all those heroes of faith that are listed in Hebrews chapter 11—Abel, Abraham, Isaac, Jacob, Joseph,

Moses and a host of others? Certainly we can learn from them and be encouraged by their example, because: "And all these, having obtained a good testimony through faith, did not receive the promise, God having provided something better for us, that they should not be made perfect apart from us" (Hebrews 11:39-40).

- They received a good testimony.
- They did **not** receive the promise.
- God has provided something better for us.

As wonderful as these heroes of faith were, they did not receive the promise. If we want to receive God's promise, we better not follow those who didn't receive. Our focus should be to discover the "something better" which God has provided for us.

How was it that all those who lived before the resurrection of Jesus Christ did not receive the promise? Didn't God answer their prayers? Didn't God bless the people who lived before Jesus? Yes, of course, they were blessed by the grace of God. The word "promise" is not talking about incidents when God answered prayer. It is referring to something much bigger. The promise is Jesus Christ Himself, coming to the earth, and coming to live in us by the Holy Spirit. Jesus referenced this before He went back to heaven: Behold, I send **the Promise** of My Father upon you; but tarry in the city of Jerusalem until you are endued with power from on high" (Luke 24:49).

In his second book, Luke refers again to the promise of the Father: "And being assembled together with them, He commanded them not to depart from Jerusalem, but to wait for **the Promise of the Father"** (Acts 1:4).

The finish line, when God's promise to humankind would be completely fulfilled, was when the Holy Spirit would be available to everyone. And the function of the Holy Spirit is to remind us of Jesus Christ and His life in us. The Holy Spirit brings to our attention that Jesus Christ is the author and finisher of faith. No wonder the apostle Paul said that he lived "by the faith of the Son of God." The only way that Simon Peter could explain the astounding miracle of a man who had been lame from birth being suddenly healed was by attributing the miracle to the faith of Jesus Christ at work:

And His name, through faith in His name, has made this man strong, whom you see and know. Yes, the faith which comes through Him has given him this perfect soundness in the presence of you all. (Acts 3:16)

It must have astounded the people in Jerusalem. The same faith that they had seen through Jesus was now in Simon Peter. Simon was still Simon and Jesus was still Jesus, and yet the faith of Jesus was expressing itself through Simon.

You will always be you, and Jesus will be Jesus. The real faith is seen when Jesus expresses Himself through you. Or, you could say that the real faith is shown when we yield ourselves and allow Jesus to flow through us. How liberating to discover that not only do we have faith in Jesus Christ, but we have the faith of Jesus Christ.

This is why Jesus told the disciples, "Have the faith of God" (Mark 11:22).

When I look back at all the years when I tried to have faith, I realize I wasn't very good at it. I wanted so much to believe, but my mind was shouting words of doubt, "what if nothing happens?" My problem was that I had faith and unbelief at the same time. Jesus said "only believe," which leaves no room for unbelief. Obviously I was disqualified. And the more I begged and pleaded with God, the less it happened.

Somehow I thought that faith would come as a result of intense pursuit after God, or spending enough time reading the Bible. I'm not suggesting that prayer and Bible reading are not important. The perceptive reader will notice that I put a premium on the Bible. After all I quote a lot of Scriptures in this book, so I obviously value the Bible. However no amount of Bible reading or prayer can earn faith. A gift must be free or it's not a gift. Faith is a gift from God, or else we could take credit for it (Ephesians 2:8-9).

In one instance in Scripture, Jesus met a father whose son was a deaf mute and taken over by evil spirits. First Jesus' disciples tried to heal the boy, but they failed. Jesus tells the father that "all things are possible to him who believes," and the father responds by telling Jesus that he believes, but he also has unbelief.

I often see this saying of Jesus misquoted. Instead of "to him" who believes, it often says all things are possible "to those" who believe. To be clear, Jesus' exact words were: "Everything is possible for him who believes" (Mark 9:23, NIV).

Who, in this account in Mark chapter 9, believed? Was it the disciples? No, Jesus makes it clear that they didn't believe. Did the father believe? Again, the father stated that he believed, but at the same time he also had unbelief. We would call that a double-minded person, who according to another Scripture doesn't receive anything from God. Did the demon-possessed, deaf mute boy believe? He doesn't seem to qualify either, because he was in an unconscious state, foaming at the mouth, rolling back and forth.

Who believed?

There's only one possible answer—**Jesus Christ believed!**

The "him" that is referred to is Jesus. The same holds true today. As long as I am trying to believe, I find that my mind is bombarded by fearful thoughts of unbelief. The change happens when I surrender to Jesus Christ and ask that His faith would flow through me. I know that I cannot muster the sufficient amount of faith, the kind of faith that only believes and doesn't doubt, so I reckon myself dead to my own ability to produce faith and alive to the faith of Jesus Christ.

Let Jesus live big in you!

Let Jesus express His faith through you!

Real faith is never panicky, but calm. Look at how Jesus approached the father with the demon-possessed boy:

"Bring him to Me." Then they brought him to Him. And when he saw Him, immediately the spirit convulsed him, and he fell on the ground and wallowed, foaming at the mouth. So He asked his father, "How long has this been happening to him?" And he said, "From childhood." (Mark 9:20-21)

Notice Jesus' calm demeanor. No panic! Just a peaceful conversation with the father, even as his son is rolling on the ground. Real faith is stress free. The story ends with the boy being healed. Jesus showed what real faith is, and that faith of Jesus is now available to us.

FOUR

Two with "Great Faith"

There are many individuals in the Gospels who are described as having faith, but only two with "great faith."

Jesus entered His hometown of Capernaum and a Roman military official approached Him, "Lord, my servant is lying at home, paralyzed and dreadfully tormented." Jesus immediately responded, "I will come and heal him." The Roman centurion couldn't ask for more than that. Jesus was completely willing and available to visit his home. The centurion responded, "Lord, I am not worthy that You should come under my roof. But only speak a word, and my servant will be healed. For I also am a man under authority, having soldiers under me. And I say to this one, 'Go,' and he goes; and to another, 'Come,' and he comes; and to my servant,

'Do this,' and he does it." Jesus marveled at the centurion's words, "Assuredly, I say to you, I have not found such <u>great faith</u>, not even in Israel!" (Matthew 8:8-10).

The account concludes with Jesus saying, "Go your way; and as you have believed, so let it be done for you. And his servant was healed that same hour" (Matthew 8:13).

Jesus "marveled," which means to "gaze in wonder." He was astonished at the faith of this Roman soldier. Jesus was unaccustomed to this kind of faith, and He had never seen it in Israel.

The second person with great faith is found a few chapters later in the Gospel of Matthew:

> Then Jesus went out from there and departed to the region of Tyre and Sidon. And behold, a woman of Canaan came from that region and cried out to Him, saying, "Have mercy on me, O Lord, Son of David! My daughter is severely demon-possessed." But He answered her not a word. And His disciples came and urged Him, saying, "Send her away, for she cries out after us." But He answered and said, "I was not sent except to the lost sheep of the house of Israel." Then she came and worshiped Him, saying, "Lord, help me!" But He answered and said, "It is not good to take the children's bread and throw it to the little dogs." And she said, "Yes, Lord, yet even the little dogs eat the crumbs which fall from their masters' table." Then Jesus answered and said to her, "O woman, <u>great is your faith</u>! Let it be to you as you desire." And her daughter was healed from that very hour. (Matthew 15:21-28)

Again Jesus states, "Great is your faith." What was it about this desperate woman that constituted extraordinary faith? Are there differences between her and the Roman centurion? What are the common denominators? How can we learn from them?

Before we answer these questions, let's look at what "great faith" is not. If we look for faith in the wrong direction, we'll come up empty. I don't claim to know everything. I know that I am nothing in myself, but the Lord Jesus Christ has poured this understanding of faith into my heart by His grace. Yes, I have witnessed thousands of healings, but I am also keenly aware of those whose prayers seem to go unanswered and I have wondered, "Why?" There doesn't seem to be any difference in the sincerity between those who receive their healing and those who seemed to walk away with their prayers unanswered. I heard many explanations and tried to come up with some myself. Well-meaning people asked me, "Peter, why do a lot more miracles happen overseas?" I never agreed with the question because I have visited many churches overseas, seeing no more happen there than I've witnessed in North America or Europe. God is not greater in one location than another. Furthermore I have seen great miracles in Europe and North America.

"The faith level is just too low," is another logical explanation that I have heard. I recall preachers who recommend to a sick person, "You must read more healing books and listen to more teaching tapes on faith." I have given the same advice. Still inwardly, I knew something was missing.

You will discover that the key to faith is to cease from all our pursuits after faith, and instead connect with Him who is our faith, Jesus Christ, the author and finisher of faith (Hebrews 12:2). This is what chapter 3 was all about. As you allow the Holy Spirit to minister this to your heart, the faith of Jesus will increasingly flow through you. In Him you will find the answers that you may have sought for a long time.

Much has been made of the fact that the Roman centurion was "under authority" because he said, "I also am a man under authority." The topic of spiritual authority is crucial and I don't want to minimize that. When we teach spiritual leadership, we focus on the truth that to have authority one must be under authority. To be a leader, one has to learn how to be a good follower. However, our study here is not leadership, but faith that works. The centurion was not making a statement about spiritual leadership. He only described how he saw his own authority as an illustration of Jesus' authority. Just like a military commander speaks and the soldiers obey, so Jesus speaks and sickness, demons and circumstances must obey!

To claim that somehow the centurion attained his miracle by understanding the need for submission to authority is false and not in line with what this account tells us. I can prove this by looking at the Canaanite woman. She appears void of any understanding of submission to authority. Actually, she seems rebellious. When Jesus at first ignores her request for a miracle, she refuses to submit to Jesus' silence. When the disciples urged Jesus, "Send her away for she cries after us," again she doesn't get the hint (Matthew 15:23). She was a nuisance to the disciples. They wanted her to leave, but she refused to come under the disciples' "authority."

I'm not suggesting we should rebel against authority;

not at all. I'm merely pointing out that whether a person has been under human authority or not does not qualify or disqualify someone to receive a blessing from God. Let me be quick to say again that I believe in authority. In our ministry we practice submitting to authority. When I visit a local church, I submit to the leader in charge of that congregation. Submitting to authority, whether spiritual or governmental, is scriptural.

Let me remove a weight from you, my sick or needy friend. Maybe you have struggled to receive a miracle from God, and when it seemed elusive you condemned yourself, blaming the lack of result on some inadequacy on your part. Possibly you blamed the lack of answered prayer on some flaw in your past. Maybe you lived a rebellious lifestyle and now you view this as an obstacle to God's blessings. The answers to your prayers will never come by looking to your failures or past shortcomings. When you look at yourself, you will only distance yourself from God's provision.

Some have suggested that the Canaanite woman's "great faith" was her insistence, pushing for her miracle against all odds. This idea of "pushing for your breakthrough," or "pressing in," or "pressing through," has been presented to many needy persons. In the case of seriously sick or dying individuals, this emphasis can be dangerous. Imagine a dying person being carried into a healing service. The person has tried every means of recovery—doctors, medicines and natural remedies. In spite of all efforts the doctor has pronounced the death sentence: "You only have a month to live." This desperate person now hears that in order to receive a miracle from God, you must push for your breakthrough, take a stand against unbelief and break the power of fear in your life. While these statements may be well-intentioned, this focus becomes a heavy burden for an already desperate person.

I propose to you that the key to the miracle of this Canaanite woman was <u>not</u> her "pushing for a breakthrough." The evidence of this is found in the account of the Roman centurion. He did not push for a miracle at all. On the contrary, he was relaxed, even laid back. Jesus offered to come to his house and heal the servant. Should not the centurion have "pushed" with all his might for Jesus to come to his house as a sure way to healing for his servant? Instead, he knew Jesus is so great that it would be enough if He would "speak the word only."

Being pushy for your blessing or miracle is not wrong or right in and of itself. I'm merely showing it is not a common denominator for "great faith." The Canaanite woman was pushy; the Roman centurion was not. If anything, being pushy or demanding in your approach to God may indicate a sense of panic, and faith and panic never work together.

Maybe you have blamed your lack of receiving on not pushing hard enough for your miracle. You condemn yourself for not trying hard enough. This may have become a burden around your neck as you push yourself ever harder to obtain a blessing. Perhaps you are struggling, shouting rebukes at the devil and faith commands at yourself, and still nothing is happening. Be at rest, there is a better way. You can have great faith, but it doesn't come by your effort, struggles or your spiritual performance. Let the weight of human inadequacy fall from you. No miracle of God has ever come because of what we strive to do.

To insist or push in your own strength for God to give you something is counterproductive. Every outstanding miracle I have witnessed has come with great peace. There's never been the case of us rolling up our "spiritual" sleeves and getting into heavy-duty boisterous screaming and rebuking of the devil. When we try to make a miracle happen, we come up empty, just like Jesus' disciples who fished all night and caught nothing. Our own efforts don't produce results. Instead, we are left disappointed, with perplexing questions and at times physically exhausted.

If I were to draw a single truth about faith out of these experiences that I have witnessed of God's healing power touching people, it would be that the greater the peace and the rest, the more people receive from God. The less we struggle, the more actually happens; and the more we try to make it happen, the less we see tangible results.

Interestingly, we find some contradictions between the behavior of the Roman centurion and the Canaanite woman. One was pushy; the other one was laid back. One seemed to understand submission to authority; the other one did not. Yet neither of these characteristics seemed to have any bearing on their ability to have great faith. Now let's look at what these two with "great faith" have in common.

FIVE

Great Faith is a Great Jesus

The middle-aged man beside me was excited. He had been blind for several years and now Jesus had opened his eyes. The crowd in the soccer stadium in northern Papua, New Guinea, listened intently before they responded with shouts of joy. When I asked the man, "Did you get healed during the prayer here tonight?" it became even more intriguing. He responded, "No, I was healed last night in my kitchen at home. You see, Mr. Youngren, I live in a village and many of the people from my area were here at your Gospel Festival. When they returned home they were excitedly reporting what God had done. I was so overwhelmed at their report that after they left my house

I simply called out, 'Jesus, come and heal me now.' Right there all by myself I was healed, and I thought I should come and report to you what Jesus did."

That man had faith, but what exactly was that faith? He took the limits off Jesus as he looked beyond the preacher and discovered the greatness of Jesus. His healing was not limited to our meeting in the stadium where I was preaching. Instead, it was all about Jesus.

The greater Jesus is to you, the greater your faith. All evidence indicates that the people who received miracles in the Gospels did not know they had faith. The two to whom "great faith" was ascribed were equally ignorant. Nowhere do we see an example of someone approaching Jesus saying, "Lord, I have faith in You, so now go ahead and heal me." This is just like the man in Papua, New Guinea. He was not concerned about having great faith; his only focus was how great Jesus is.

Have we put such focus on acquiring faith that people are seeking it, rather than pursuing the Source of faith?

Faith doesn't come by seeking after faith; it comes from Jesus.

Paul writes, "So then faith comes by hearing, and hearing by the word of God" (Romans 10:17). When you look in the context you see that the "hearing" referred to is when we hear of Jesus Christ and His death and resurrection. We are saved when we believe in our heart that God raised Jesus from the dead (v. 9). Do you see how faith is connected to Jesus? It is not isolated to believing in a word, idea or doctrine.

Faith is directly connected to the person of Jesus. The word we hear, which builds our faith, is the word about Jesus Christ and what He has done.

Faith is not in your mind; it is in your heart. When we willingly come to Jesus Christ, He imparts His faith to us. It is two sides of the same coin. On the one hand, Jesus is our faith. On the other hand, when we come to Him, He imparts His faith to us. We are saved by grace through faith. Faith is not of ourselves or from our effort; it is a gift of God (Ephesians 2:8-9). This idea is revolutionary. If this truth sinks into our hearts, faith will never again be the same to us.

In chapter 3 of this book, we looked at Hebrews chapter 11, where we see a long list of "faith heroes." I noted that sometimes this chapter has been called, "Faith's Hall of Fame." Abel, Enoch, Noah, Abraham, Sarah, Isaac, Jacob, Joseph, Moses and others are given as examples of faith. What constituted faith for these "faith heroes"? Faith to them was obedience to a divine word. Amazingly, we are never told anywhere to imitate these "faith heroes." Some have looked at Hebrews chapter 11 and struggled to live up to the achievements of these great men and women of the past. On the contrary, the chapter ends, "And all these, having obtained a good testimony through faith, did not receive the promise, God having provided *something better* for us, that they should not be made perfect apart from us" (Hebrews 11:39-40).

Let's look at little deeper at this phrase *"something better."* As we already noted, the definition of that which is better comes one verse later, "Looking unto Jesus, the author and finisher of (our) faith…" (Hebrews 12:2). The Old

Testament people are commendable for how they obeyed a divine word; however, this is not the way we exercise faith. We have a better way. We connect directly with the indwelling Christ in us (Colossians 1:27).

This truth of "something better" is in line with the theme of the whole Book of Hebrews, where the key word is "better." Jesus is better than the angels, and better than Aaron and Moses. The voice of God's Son is better than the voice of the prophets, and His blood is better than that of goats and calves. We have a better High Priest than the one in the Old Testament, and the New Covenant is better than the one which came through Moses. This doesn't mean that the angels, Aaron, or the blood of goats and calves were bad. The writer of Hebrews doesn't suggest that the prophets were evil or bad; not in the least. All of these had their place, but Jesus is better.

There is no indication that the writer of Hebrews is suddenly changing the theme when he comes to chapter 11. The list of Old Testament heroes is given in contrast to that which is better. We don't exercise faith the way they did because we have something better—we have the faith of Jesus. This is not a critique of the Old Testament heroes. On the contrary, they believed God according to what was available in their time, but our time is different. We live after the death and resurrection of Christ. Faith is "better" now. We have much more than a divine word; *we have Jesus Himself.*

Religion has made this difficult for many people to embrace. We are accustomed to see God far away, off in the distance, somewhere else. That's why it's easier for us to talk about faith in Christ, because it seems that Christ is still out there away from us. Obviously if Christ lives in us, then we have the faith of Christ. Faith *in* Christ is good, but the faith *of* Christ is greater. That's why the apostle Paul stated that we "live by the faith of the Son of God" (Galatians 2:20). This Scripture from Paul's letter to the Galatians is so key to everything in a Christian life that for many years I had it displayed on a large billboard at the entrance-way into my office. I knew that I needed to be reminded that Christ is my life. Some may have recognized that Christ is our righteousness, our wisdom and our sanctification. I'm glad to add to that, Christ is also our faith. Faith is not in an idea or a concept, it is completely wrapped up in the person of Jesus Christ.

Since we are crucified with Christ, and a "crucified" person is dead, our only hope is that the life of another is lived through us. We have been crucified with Jesus Christ, and now He lives in us with His wisdom, faith and love. This is the awesome key to the entire life of a believer in Jesus. We have become new creations in Christ (2 Corinthians 5:17). Sometimes we talk about salvation in terms of us giving our life to Christ. That's not really true. The truth is that Christ imparts His life to us. We are recreated in the image of God. Our life can never please God, but we have died from the old life.

When the apostle Simon Peter called it "the faith which comes through Him" (Acts 3:16), he recognized that faith was not the product of his own effort. No, the miracle-working faith Simon Peter experienced was all wrapped up in Jesus; faith which "comes through Him."

The greater Jesus is to you, the greater your faith.

If your faith seems small, focus on Jesus more. The Roman centurion and the Canaanite woman had a great Jesus. The centurion thought Jesus was so great that "a word" from Him would be enough. Though Jesus had already offered to come to the centurion's home, the centurion recommended otherwise. Why? He obviously thought Jesus is so great that a potentially arduous journey was unnecessary. Instead, "a word" was sufficient. It is as if the centurion was saying, "Jesus, You're so great; You don't have to come to my house. Just like I speak to a subordinate to go and he goes, come and he comes, when You release Your word, the sickness in my servant must leave."

The centurion had come for *healing*, but instead he saw *the Healer*. Jesus was so much greater than he could have ever imagined. All around there were those who wanted to limit Jesus saying things like, "We know Jesus. He's from Nazareth. He's Joseph's son, nothing special." In that sea of unbelief and negative comments, the centurion's voice rises above all others. He sees Jesus for who He really is.

Look at the Canaanite woman. At first, Jesus doesn't respond to her request for the healing of her daughter. He states, "I was not sent except to the lost sheep of the house of Israel" (Matthew 15:24). When the woman keeps insisting that her daughter must be healed, Jesus responds, "It is not good to take the children's bread and throw it to the little dogs" (Matthew 15:26).

Jesus was still operating within the context of the Old Testament—"the house of Israel." The gospel had not yet gone global. That would come after Jesus' death, resurrection, exaltation to heaven and the outpouring of the promised Holy Spirit. There is a clear delineation between the Old and the New Covenant. The woman is not Jewish and consequently not a part of God's covenant with the Jewish people. We who live today don't have to be concerned about this distinction. After Jesus' death and resurrection, all distinctions are erased. Now all, whether Jew or Gentile, have access to God by the same covenant, the better covenant of Jesus Christ.

Jesus tells the woman that healing is the "bread of the children." Bread is a basic food. Healings and miracles are basic to those who embrace God's covenant in Jesus.

This woman could have been insulted by Jesus' seeming disinterest. In fact, Jesus' love was flowing toward her, but at the same time Jesus was respecting the fact that He was still in the Old Covenant. Jesus also knew that anyone, Jew or Gentile, could be healed by faith. You who read this don't need to be concerned about the Old and the New Covenant. You are in the New Covenant, and the blessings of that covenant are yours. The important point for us to consider is how great Jesus was to the Canaanite woman.

She saw a great Jesus, and Jesus saw "great faith."

The Canaanite woman refused to be offended. Her response demonstrates how great Jesus was to her. She exclaims, "Yes, Lord, yet even the little dogs eat the crumbs which fall from their masters' table" (Matthew 15:27).

Jesus' answer to her about healing being "bread of the

children" may not have been the response she hoped for, but it was what she got; and she took it. It is as if she thought, "Well, I didn't get the answer I wanted, but Jesus said something, and I know His word is so reliable He will never back off from what He said!" Using Jesus' own expression, she makes it clear she doesn't need the whole loaf or even a slice of this "bread." To her, Jesus is so great that a "crumb" is sufficient.

Great faith is not found in looking for great faith. Great faith is a great Jesus.

See Him as great as He is. See His redemptive work and His power and love for you.

Faith doesn't come by trying. If you try to have faith and feel success in obtaining it, I regrettably inform you that what you have is not real faith. You may have a feeling of faith. You may talk like you would if you had real faith, but it's not the real faith. That kind of faith comes not from trying to get it—it comes from Jesus Himself.

This is so simple that many miss it altogether. Call on Jesus. Ask for His help. He will not fail you. Don't rely on theological beliefs or your years of Christian service. Approach Jesus like a child would his parent, expecting that He will give you mercy.

SIX

Faith or Mental Believing

There is a huge gap between mental believing and the God-kind of faith. Mental believing is natural. It comes by repeatedly telling our mind it is so. True faith is supernatural. It moves mountains and is only found in Jesus.

The four Gospels give us many case studies that contrast mental believing with the God-kind of faith. We looked briefly in an earlier chapter at the story of Jesus healing the demon-possessed boy. Now let's go a little deeper. Matthew chapter 17 begins with Jesus and three of His disciples on the Mount of Transfiguration. When they come down from the mountain, Jesus quickly encounters human pain and suffering. We read, "And when they had come to the multitude, a man came to Him, kneeling down to Him and saying, 'Lord,

71

have mercy on my son, for he is an epileptic and suffers severely; for he often falls into the fire and often into the water. So I brought him to Your disciples, but they could not cure him'" (Matthew 17:14-16).

Can you see the desperation? It's obvious Jesus' disciples believed in healing, otherwise they would not have tried to cure the boy. The father must have also believed in the miracle-working power of Jesus, because later he says, "Lord, I believe; help my unbelief!" (Mark 9:24)

We don't know all the details, but we can well imagine the disciples gathered around the boy while he was rolling on the ground, foaming at the mouth. Maybe they rebuked the devil or commanded the demons to leave and nothing happened. Possibly they tried repeatedly praying, interceding and pleading with God. Maybe they encouraged the father to believe more fervently, putting the onus for more faith on him or on the boy. Did the disciples try to discern the cause of the boy's sickness? Maybe they tried to research what had been the entry point for the demons to begin to oppress the boy and his family. We don't know exactly how they attempted to cure the boy, but we know they tried. Still, after all the prayer, rebuking and crying out to God was done, the result was dismal. The boy was as sick as ever before. Now some may conclude that this indicated it was not God's will to heal the boy. We know that's not the case because, when Jesus came, He said, "Bring him here to Me" (Matthew 17:17). After a short conversation with the father, Jesus heals the boy. Jesus' action proves that it was God's will to heal the boy.

Later on, the disciples wonder at what they have seen and why they could not cure the boy. Jesus explains, "Because of your unbelief; for assuredly, I say to you, if you have faith as a mustard seed, you will say to this mountain, 'Move from here to there,' and it will move; and nothing will be impossible for you" (Matthew 17:20).

Do you see the distinction between mental believing and mountain-moving faith? The disciples had exercised mental believing. No question! They believed that healing was to be expected, or they would not have attempted to cure the boy. Jesus shows real faith in contrast to the mental believing, exhibited by the disciples. He explains to them that they only need a mustard seed of the real kind of faith, and the miracle will happen.

A billion dollars of mental believing and nothing will happen, but a penny of faith, the God-kind of faith, and everything is possible.

What we call "faith" is often only mental believing, or "mind over matter." Sometimes when people are struggling to receive healing, or some other blessing from the Lord, they may be heard repeatedly saying, "I'm healed, I'm healed, I'm healed," or "I got it, I got it, I got it," or "It's mine, it's mine, it's mine." It is as if we thought that by repeating something enough, we'll convince our own minds that we believe it, and then we'll get it.

The faith that Jesus gives, the God-kind of faith, is alive, vibrant and powerful. Let's never reduce faith to "five steps, ten keys, seven clues, or ten secrets." Faith can never be reduced to a mere principle or a "step." It is much more than affirming a doctrine; it is the energy of Jesus Himself flowing through you. Faith is not a condition of our mind; it is a divine grace.

A truckload of mental believing produced by human effort and struggle will do nothing, but a teaspoonful of the faith of Jesus will move mountains every time. The good news is that Jesus makes this faith readily available. You only have to come to Him, call out for Him, and draw near to Him. "But as many as received <u>Him</u>, to them <u>He</u> gave the right to become children of God, to those who believe in <u>His</u> name" (John 1:12). It's all wrapped up in "Him," "He" and "His." He does the work and we receive the benefits.

In every Billy Graham crusade, when the invitation for people to come to Christ was given, the choir would sing, "Just as I am without one plea, but that Thy blood was shed for me." Those words, "without one plea," can be applied to all areas of our relationship with God. They simply mean that I have nothing to plead of my own, there's nothing I can do to merit God's gift. I cannot brag of a single good thing about myself, including boasting of my faith. Instead, I simply come, just as I am, asking for God's mercy.

Remember the prayer meeting in the temple in Jerusalem with the publican in the back crying out for mercy, and the self-righteous Pharisee in the front of the sanctuary thanking God that he was not as "other sinners." Whose shoes would you rather be in: the publican sinner or the self-righteous Pharisee? There is no blessing in coming to God presenting something of ourselves, but mercy and grace flowed freely to the one who came "without one plea." All our mental attempts at faith will avail nothing. When we come to Jesus without anything of our own, the floodgates of His mercy and love open wide to us.

On another occasion Jesus and the disciples were in a

boat, and a raging storm threatened to drown them. The disciples were on the deck crying out to God to save them, but the storm continued unabated. Obviously they believed that God could calm the storm, or they would not have been praying. Yet, this falls under the category of mental believing. Jesus slept through the storm, but when the disciple woke Him up He simply spoke the words, "Peace be still" and there was a great calm (Mark 4:39). Here we see the contrast between the mental believing of the disciples and the faith which comes of Jesus. The disciples spared no effort to believe to see something happen, but to no avail. Then Jesus comes with real faith and everything changes. I have discovered that I can exert myself in prayer, begging for God to do something, and yet nothing happens. Then when I become still on the inside, focusing on God's love for me and what Jesus Christ has done for me, faith is there as an inner confidence. Then when I speak, I'm not merely expressing a wish or trying to get God to do something, but instead I'm speaking with full assurance that what I need is already done by Jesus Christ.

Someone may ask, "Isn't it important that we speak words of faith?"

Yes, faith speaks and confesses God's Word. Keep in mind that the Living Word is Jesus Christ Himself, so to confess God's Word is to confess Jesus Christ and what He has done. Some have made a mistake in just confessing various Scripture verses, without seeing those verses connected to Jesus' finished work. In order for our positive confession of God's Word to work, it has to be anchored in Jesus Christ. When the real faith is present, we confess on the basis of what

Christ has done for us, but faith doesn't come from positive confession, for faith comes from Jesus. That's why the Scripture says, "I believe, therefore I spoke," not, "I spoke until I believed."

You may ask, "Is it important that we take steps of faith, that we act in faith?"

Yes, action comes from faith, not faith from action—for faith only comes from Jesus.

While preaching in the central square in Plovdiv, Bulgaria, a mother brought her five-year-old son, Vasco, who had been born paralyzed. The mother had heard of the wonders of Jesus that had happened in our previous meeting in Sofia, the capital of Bulgaria. She was overwhelmed with what she had heard, and now certain that her son would walk, she bought him a pair of jeans, a jean jacket and a brand new pair of sneakers. The boy had never owned a pair of shoes; he had no need for them as he could neither stand nor walk. However, Vasco's mother was sure he would need shoes because Jesus would heal him. As I preached Jesus that night, a beaming five-year-old and a crying mother came on the platform. Vasco ran back and forth showing the people the wonder that had happened. The people were beside themselves with joy. That's the faith of Jesus in operation. He gave Vasco's mother mountain-moving faith.

Now I could tell that story and someone else who was lame could also buy new shoes and come to a meeting and nothing would happen. To the one person this was a living, vibrant reality. To another person it may only be another faith technique.

Faith is not a method; faith is a Person.

In one of our Gospel Festivals in India, a man paralyzed from his waist down was lying on the ground listening as I spoke of Jesus Christ. He pushed himself up, leaning on his arms, all the while inching his way around the crowd to get a closer view of the platform. When I spoke in the name of Jesus for the lame to rise up and walk, he tried to get up but fell down. He did it again with the same dismal result. I would never have known these details unless a friend of mine, Pastor Frederick Mwassa from the east coast of Kenya, had been present. He was standing looking at this pitiful sight of a man trying to get up and walk. He told me after the meeting, "Peter, I approached the lame man saying, 'Shall I help you?' The man responded, 'No, I believe the word of Jesus that I have heard preached. I believe it more than I believe in my paralyzed condition. I will walk on my own.'" Again he tried, and this time life flowed to his limbs. He jumped to his feet and came running to the platform while all the people who'd seen him began to weep and cry, beside themselves at what they had just witnessed. The Holy Spirit had revealed Jesus to that man. Jesus had given him faith, and no one was going to talk him out of it.

I could relate this story, and another person in a similar condition could say and act in exactly the same way, and nothing would happen. It is true that faith responds by acting, that faith without works is dead. But faith doesn't come from imitating the action of someone else; faith comes from Jesus. Don't try to imitate or copy what someone else has done, instead focus on Jesus. Ask the Holy Spirit to reveal

Jesus to you more every day. Jesus' faith, assurance and peace will come into your heart. This is why every miracle testimony is unique, whether a testimony from the Bible or a current one. As each individual connects with Jesus, that person will act out his or her faith in Him. Jesus is the key to everything. Our miracle is in Him.

The more we look at our own effort, the worse it gets, while the more we look at Jesus, the easier it becomes.

I have increasingly made my whole focus to lift up Jesus. The apostle Paul writes, "O foolish Galatians! Who has bewitched you that you should not obey the truth, before whose eyes Jesus Christ was clearly portrayed among you as crucified?" (Galatians 3:1). Faith, miracles, healings and wonders are not produced by methods or faith techniques. These blessings come when people fully see Jesus portrayed. This was Paul's preaching style: to vividly paint a picture of the awesomeness of Jesus.

Mental believing comes from within our self. We try to achieve a level of mental concentration where we think we believe something. This is the complete opposite of the faith of God. Look again at this Scripture. "For by grace you have been saved through faith, and that not of yourselves; it is the gift of God, not of works, lest anyone should boast" (Ephesians 2:8-9).

This means:

1. *Faith is "not of ourselves"*;
2. *Faith is "a gift of God"*;
3. *Faith is "not of work"*;

4. *If faith came from ourselves or our works, we could boast, but since it doesn't, all boasting goes to Jesus.*

The next verse sheds light on how real faith comes. "For we are His workmanship, created in Christ Jesus for good works, which God prepared beforehand that we should walk in them" (Ephesians 2:10). Everything we have is because we are new creations in Christ Jesus. We are believers because Jesus Christ, the Author and Finisher of faith, is in us. *We nurture and grow this God-given faith by continually looking unto Jesus.*

Do you work for a "gift"? Obviously not! A gift must be free or it is no longer a gift. Faith is a gift of God. At times we hear people say, "I have seriously studied and prayed and my faith is growing. I believe I can do great things for God now." This type of speaking is an indication that faith's not at work, because we cannot work for faith and consequently we can't boast in it.

Now, don't misunderstand me. I practice Bible reading, prayer, and spiritual discipline with all my heart. Still we may read and pray diligently and yet not have the faith that moves mountains. Only Jesus gives us this faith. When His peaceful presence touches us, another world will open up to us. It's no longer us trying to have faith. Instead, His faith, the faith of Jesus, is flowing through us. He is our TOTAL MIRACLE SOURCE.

Some have misconstrued this teaching and suggested that good works are not important. We see in the verse I quoted above that we are "created for good works." The Bible draws a distinction between "dead works" (Hebrews

6:1) and good works. The dead works are our own futile attempts to do religious and spiritual deeds in order to obtain favor or blessing from God. This is the opposite of faith. However, once we recognize Christ's life in us, we will step into the good works that God has prepared for us. These will not be works that we can brag about or take credit for, but rather it will be Christ working through us.

SEVEN

Faith Flourishes by Grace

Great faith cannot function under pressure to perform or live up to requirements. As long as the sick or needy person is evaluating: "Am I good enough? Have I prayed enough? Fasted enough? Read the Bible enough? Have I shown enough Christian virtues?" faith becomes paralyzed. Often sick people will question and look for hindrances to their healing. Many try to find something wrong by digging into their past or failures. This short-circuits the operation of faith.

The New Testament draws a stark distinction between grace and law.

Grace is what God has done for us. Law is what we try to do.

81

Grace is the undeserved, unearned, unmerited favor of God given to us because of Jesus. It is totally focused on God's love providing a free gift to everyone who believes through Jesus Christ. The law focuses on human performance and how much good we can do. As long as we look at ourselves and our works, we will fall short.

Let's look again at the Roman centurion and the Canaanite woman, the only people to whom Jesus ascribed "great faith." Who were they? They were Gentiles, or non-Jewish, which means they were not under the Law of Moses. Not only were they not under the Law of Moses, in all likelihood, they were completely ignorant of the law. Let me show you how faith cannot operate in combination with the law.

The word "faith" is only used twice in the Old Testament; once as a rebuke of the people of Israel (Deuteronomy 32:20), and once in a prophetic promise pertaining to the life of a believer in Jesus (Habakkuk 2:4). The Old Testament was the era of law and rules, and faith can never coexist with the religious works. Faith and religious works are diametrically opposed.

The apostle Paul shows the difference between faith and law. In chapter 3, we looked at Jesus as the author and finisher of faith. Let's look again at the first Scripture verse that I referenced in that teaching: "But before faith came, we were kept under guard by the law, kept for the faith which would afterward be revealed. Therefore the law was our tutor to bring us to Christ, that we might be justified by faith. But after faith has come, we are no longer under a tutor" (Galatians 3:23-25).

I underlined the words "before" and "afterward." These

words indicate a specific time. Faith came at a specific time. We know that specific time—it was at the resurrection of Jesus. In order to be saved we must believe that God raised Jesus from the dead (Romans 10:9). Until Jesus rose from the dead such faith was not possible. That's why the New Covenant begins with the resurrection of Jesus. Before that time the law was in effect, but once faith had come, the law was no longer necessary.

What is the law? How does it relate to us today? Without giving a lengthy historical analysis, the law is about what <u>we</u> can do. It has to do with self-effort, human performance and living up to a standard that "qualifies" us for God's blessings. The people of Israel tried this and failed miserably.

God's objective with the law was to show the human inability to live according to God's holy and perfect commandments. Simon Peter said that neither the Pharisees nor their forefathers had been able to comply with God's law no matter how hard they tried (Acts 15:10). As the law showed us our inability to live up to God's standard, it also prepared us to be willing to receive grace. The more we see our inability, the more grace becomes our only hope.

Grace is the unmerited, unearned, undeserved favor of God toward people.

"<u>Unmerited</u>" means grace doesn't come by achievements or good things we have done. Being a leader, a pastor or bishop doesn't qualify us for grace. It doesn't come by merit.

"<u>Unearned</u>" indicates that grace is not by our own effort, studies or hard work. Nothing we do can possibly earn us God's blessings.

"Undeserved" simply means that we are unworthy in ourselves of God's favor. If we feel we deserve a blessing, miracle or divine favor, we have, in a sense, disqualified ourselves from that grace.

Faith and law cannot mix. Meanwhile, grace and faith flow together. "For by grace you have been saved through faith, and that not of yourselves; it is the gift of God, not of works, lest anyone should boast" (Ephesians 2:8-9). Do you see how faith is the opposite of human performance?

Let's dissect what we read in Galatians 3:23-25:

1. *The law was "before faith came" (v. 23);*
2. *The law was only until Christ came (v. 24);*
3. *When Jesus came, faith came. Faith is now a Person. Jesus is our faith (v. 23-25);*
4. *Once the Faith (Jesus Christ) has come, we no longer obtain anything from God by the law, but through faith (v. 25-26). Everything is available in and through Jesus now.*

One of the themes is this book is "great faith." We look at the Roman centurion and the Canaanite woman as the only two people to whom Jesus ascribed great faith. Here's another common denominator; neither one of them had ever been exposed to the law. They did not know the requirements necessary for a miracle.

Paul asked the Galatians, "Therefore He who supplies the Spirit to you and works miracles among you, does He do it by the works of the law, or by the hearing of faith?" (Galatians 3:5). The answer is obvious. The working of miracles was because of the hearing of faith, the hearing of Jesus Christ. Real faith cannot function under requirements, because every person, no matter how well intentioned, will fall short of those requirements. By focusing on laws and requirements we will only see our own shortcomings, while when we look at Jesus we see His abilities.

Those with great faith could only have great faith because they didn't know the requirements. They had not read, "...If you diligently obey the voice of the LORD your God, to observe carefully all His commandments which I command you today, that the LORD your God will set you high..." (Deuteronomy 28:1). Once we know that the blessing is dependent on our obedience and careful observing of "all commandments," we know we are disqualified. Who among us has obeyed all of God's Word 24/7?

We read in Joshua 1:8, "This Book of the Law shall not depart from your mouth, but you shall meditate in it day and night, that you may observe to do according to all that is written in it. For then you will make your way prosperous, and then you will have good success." Once we know that prosperity and "good success" are dependent on us speaking, meditating and observing "all that is written," and that we do it "day and night," we quickly must disqualify ourselves from the blessing of God. Is there anyone who has kept a 100% focus on God's Word? Certainly not. That is why Jesus says, "He who is without sin cast the first stone" (John 8:7).

This is the dilemma of the legalistic thinking—no one is qualified. If our miracle depends on us—that we have done enough, prayed enough, worshipped enough, read the Bible enough, and been good enough—then we must conclude that the miracle will never happen.

When we look at what we have done, faith is impossible, because faith is about what Jesus has done.

The Bible shows us that people who were not under the law received great miracles. Jesus said, "...many widows were in Israel in the days of Elijah, when...there was a great famine throughout all the land; but to none of them was Elijah sent except to Zarephath, in the region of Sidon, to a woman who was a widow. And many lepers were in Israel in the time of Elisha the prophet, and none of them was cleansed except Naaman, the Syrian" (Luke 4:25-27).

When Jesus highlighted great miracles from the Old Testament, He focused on two people who were both outside the Law of Moses: a widow without food and a leprous Syrian general. These two were also ignorant of the requirements of the law.

Faith cannot operate alongside a list of requirements. It only works through Christ. "For the Son of God, Jesus Christ, who was preached among you by us...was not Yes and No, but in Him was Yes. For *all the promises of God in Him are Yes, and in Him Amen,* to the glory of God through us" (2 Corinthians 1:19-20). "All God's promises" means everything God has ever promised. How do we receive these promises? Not by our performance, but in Christ. That way no glory goes to us, but when the miracle manifests, it is "to the glory of God through us."

This is why new believers receive so easily. They pray for a parking spot and get it. I remember, as a young traveling preacher, staying in the home of a new believer. When the pastor had asked the congregation if anyone would house the traveling minister during a week-long revival, the recently saved businessman and his wife immediately responded, thinking they would have an opportunity to learn more about God. The couple owned a furniture factory and, while I was their houseguest, several of the heavy-duty sewing machines used for upholstery broke down. To the amazement of the employees, the owner who just weeks earlier would have sworn and cursed, now laid hands on the sewing machines in Jesus' name, and somehow the sewing machines started working. It boggled my mind. These new believers received so easily.

Why is this situation a rather common scenario? New believers have not yet been told of the "requirements" for a miracle. Often when new believers pray, their only focus is Jesus who can do all things. Then one day we announce a seminar on "How to Receive from God" and we teach "Seven Steps to Victory" or "Ten Secrets to Your Breakthrough." We make the miracle complicated and soon new believers are discouraged. Suddenly the miracle is no longer focused on Jesus—it has become a formula. All too often that formula is all about us and what we must do, how much we must worship, rebuke the devil, study, pray, fast and meditate. Now the new believer realizes he should never have received any answer to prayer at all. After all, he has not lived up to the requirements. Faith is a gift from God but religion makes it a product of what we do. This completely contradicts Paul's teaching that faith does not work in conjunction with human effort.

People ask me why miracles seem to come so easily overseas. It has nothing to do with "overseas." It has everything to do with whether people have been exposed to legalism or not. Forget the myth that miracles happen overseas.

Miracles happen to people who are not under the curse of legalistic thinking.

Yes, in our Gospel Festivals we consistently see mighty miracles follow the proclamation of Jesus Christ to multitudes of non-Christians. These "unbelievers" hear a message that Jesus is able and willing to help them. I tell the people, "If you don't have faith, or if your faith is small, no problem, we'll ask Jesus to give you faith." You see, we focus only on Jesus and Him crucified. When the people believe this Christ-centered teaching, miracles happen.

Some think I preach about healings and miracles. Really, I do not. I preach about Jesus as our righteousness and what He has already done for the world and for each one of us as individuals. And miracles follow. When you preach signs, wonders and miracles you may see some results, but when you preach Jesus our righteousness, signs, wonders and miracles are the inevitable result as faith comes to the people who hear the Gospel.

The same miracles happen to people who have been Christians all their lives; if they are willing to come to God without any reliance on their own efforts. The problem is when Christians expect God to heal them because of their own faithfulness or good works. No, we all come to God like little children totally dependent on their parent.

When people ask me to pray for them, they sometimes say, "Pastor Peter, I have lots of faith." Immediately I am quite sure nothing will happen. You see, people who speak in this manner usually think they have faith based on what they have done. Maybe they prayed a lot, or listened to audio teachings about faith and healing, or read books on the subject. Real faith never looks to our own performance; it only looks to Jesus. The mountain-moving faith has nothing to do with an intellectual knowledge of doctrine. We may know about faith, miracles and healings, but this in itself does not constitute faith.

Maybe you have been inwardly measuring your faith to see if you qualify for a miracle. You will never measure up or qualify. *Look to Jesus, who has already qualified you.* You are not qualified by what you can do, but by what He <u>has</u> done.

One of the most famous miracles recorded in Scripture is the healing of blind Bartimaeus. Jesus said Bartimaeus had faith, "Go your way; your faith has made you well" (Mark 10:52). It's nice to notice that someone has faith, but even more importantly: how did he get it? Someone may suggest that Bartimaeus already had faith before Jesus came, but that does not make sense. If he had faith, he would have been healed before Jesus came, because faith always works. We must therefore conclude that before Jesus came onto the scene, Bartimaeus did not have faith that his blind eyes would open. It all started when the beggar heard that Jesus was passing by.

Bartimaeus did not recite positive words like, "I'm healed, I'm healed, I'm healed," or "I can see, I can see, I can see." He became *completely Jesus-focused.* Though some tried to discourage him suggesting it was not appropriate for him to boisterously and loudly call for Jesus, he continued all the more crying out, "Jesus, have mercy on me!" (Mark 10:48).

Jesus responded to Bartimaeus, "What do you want Me to do for you?" (Mark 10:51).

Notice, Jesus is not telling Bartimaeus anything that he should do. Instead, Jesus suggests that He will do something. Some today might have told Bartimaeus that he needed to break the spirit of fear, intimidation and blindness over his life. Others may have thought he should go back to the root of the sickness and break that, or some other spiritual exercise that Bartimaeus ought to have done. This is completely foreign to Jesus' healing approach. His question was simply, "What do you want Me to do?" Bartimaeus could obviously not do anything to be healed or he would have already done it. The healing that was about to happen was totally dependent on Jesus.

Jesus never laid a heavy burden or a legalistic thought on a sick and needy person. Instead He helped that hurting person to turn his attention away from his own inability and onto Jesus who was able to do something about the situation. Maybe you want to lift your hands and praise and give thanks to Jesus right now. Say words like, "Holy Spirit, reveal Jesus more fully to me." As you become COMPLETELY JESUS-FOCUSED, His faith begins to flourish in you.

EIGHT

Faith is Restful

Faith is easy. It is simply yielding to and resting in Jesus' ability. The apostle Paul asks the Galatian believers, "He who supplies the Spirit to you and works miracles among you, does he do it by the works of the law or by the hearing of faith?" (Galatians 3:5)

Put this question in contemporary language. Do you receive the Holy Spirit and does God work miracles among you by your efforts and struggles? Does it happen by how well you have performed your religious duties? Or do these divine blessings come by hearing of Jesus and His abilities?

As a young new believer, I heard that the next step in my spiritual growth was to receive the baptism of the Holy Spirit. Naturally, I wanted to advance in my newfound life as a believer, and I thought I must have this experience with the Holy Spirit. I was spending three weeks at a Christian youth camp where people told me that if I sincerely wanted the baptism of the Holy Spirit, I should attend a 7:00 AM prayer meeting. These were beautiful Christian friends and they wanted the best for me. They emphasized that this prayer time was only for those who were sincere in their quest for the Holy Spirit. I was fourteen years old and an early-morning prayer meeting was not really my style, but I wanted to put forth a good effort. Bleary-eyed, I rolled out of bed at five minutes to seven in the morning and rushed to the prayer meeting. We begged and pleaded with the Lord, "Please God, please baptize us in the Holy Spirit." If anyone should have received because of our effort, it should have been us. In fact, one of the young men, Hans, who was the leader of this prayer-meeting, was an exemplary youth. I felt I was not nearly as "holy" as he. He was the one who woke me up so I would make it in time to the prayer meeting. If anyone should have been rewarded with the baptism of the Holy Spirit, it was Hans. He had a stepbrother who was his complete opposite, named Steve. Steve wasn't saved, and furthermore was the number one troublemaker at the youth camp. If anything went wrong, any prank, we knew Steve was behind it.

One night this rebellious young man wandered into our evening service. We never knew if he'd show up or not, though the rules of the camp mandated that everybody had to be in attendance. Steve was crying and called out that he needed Jesus. We all thought that was wonderful. We knew he needed salvation considering what a "big sinner" he was. Fifteen minutes after Steve received Jesus as his Savior, he was baptized in the Holy Spirit speaking in other tongues. When we saw this, knowing how thoroughly unsanctified he was, we were a bit unsure. However, we thought, "Well, God is good so maybe this is all right after all." Then, twenty minutes after this experience we heard Steve's voice from the back of the auditorium speaking a message in other tongues, prefacing it with "thus says the Lord."

If you are unfamiliar with this kind of a happening, it is described in Paul's writing to the Corinthians. A message in tongues and giving its interpretation are two out of the nine gifts of the Holy Spirit mentioned there. Steve was giving a message in tongues and interpreting, prophesying to us who felt superior to him spiritually. The word he gave was very powerful, and though we sensed it was a word from God, we had a tough time receiving it. What business did God have to use such a troublemaker? If anyone should have been prophesying, it should have been one of us who had attended the 7:00 AM prayer meeting. We had been begging God and seemingly received nothing. Do you see how a religious legalistic mindset works? The legalistic condemning person hates the undeserved, unearned, unmerited favor of God. "Didn't Steve still need to get sanctified?" you may ask. Of course, but God does not give miracles according to how qualified a person is. He does it by faith. I've seen this scenario repeated hundreds of times. It's the hopeless and the hurting who are touched by Jesus.

All Christian virtues, including humility and sanctification, are very important. God's grace will work in us if we allow it to produce these qualities. However, possession of Christian virtues does not earn us points toward a miracle.

As mentioned earlier, hundreds of people have approached me saying, "Pastor Peter, pray for me. I have lots of faith. Just ask God to heal me now." I could be wrong—there could be some instance I have forgotten—but I can't think of a single person who approached me proclaiming how much faith they had who actually received their miracle. Faith is not an issue of human performance but rather of connecting a person with Jesus.

People who are focused on faith rarely receive; those focused on Jesus readily receive.

That's why the stories of the Canaanite woman and the Roman centurion are so important. Jesus ascribed "great faith" to them in spite of the fact that they seemed oblivious to any of the requirements for healing. They were Gentiles who had not been exposed to the law of Moses. The less we look at ourselves and the more we look to Jesus, the more faith comes. Faith has nothing to do with our achievement or our worthiness. Questions like, "Am I good enough? Do I measure up?" make faith of no effect.

Faith rests in Jesus and His ability. That's why we often see Muslims, Buddhists, and Hindus who know very little about the Bible receive astounding miracles. Though they have never heard of the Book of Genesis, the Epistles to the Romans or Galatians, they grasp the simple truth of God's love revealed in Jesus for them.

Once a person connects with Jesus, everything is possible.

When we forget ourselves and look at Jesus Christ, we become peaceful. Faith is not rules concerning what we must do. When we see Jesus as big as He really is, we relax in Him. When Jesus appears great to your inward eyes, you automatically start speaking positively, confessing God's Word. In fact, you can't speak negatively when you see Jesus completely as big and awesome. This is entirely opposite of being stressed to live up to expectations, as if God were a scorekeeper in heaven counting points to see if you have shown enough faith to qualify for an answer to your prayers.

Peter Youngren's self-manufactured faith is no good; that's why I hook up with Jesus' faith. If it's up to the sick person's faith or the preacher's faith, we don't have much hope. Sometimes people say to me, "Peter, you're such a man of faith." Of course, I like when people say nice things about me, but in myself I'm not a great man of faith. Truthfully, in myself I have little or no faith, but I have experienced thousands of times when Jesus' ability and His faith have flowed through me. Because of Jesus living in me, I have full access to His faith. I yield to Him.

It is stressful to pretend faith. If a doctor diagnoses that I'm going to die in thirty days, my mind understands the implications of that diagnosis. I can't psych myself into some miracle-working faith; I need the faith of the Son of God. I would want to pray, "Lord, no matter how hard I try to believe, no matter how much I try to put on a good face, I know that Your faith is the only faith that works. Jesus, I just want to draw closer to You. Let Your life, Word, faith and power flow through me."

95

When Jesus calmed the raging storm, all the disciples were on deck screaming, "We perish! God help us!" All the while Jesus was asleep in the bottom of the boat. We may have foolishly reprimanded Jesus, "Don't You have any sense of responsibility, Jesus? The boat is going under and You're asleep? At least the disciples showed some responsibility and cried for help." If we didn't know any better, we would think the disciples were the ones with faith. If the Bible account had said there were thirteen people on the boat and one was asleep, we would have thought the one sleeping was Judas or Thomas or maybe Simon Peter, but not Jesus. The Bible account, however, is clear that the author and finisher of faith was asleep on a pillow. There's no panic with Jesus.

When Jesus heard that Lazarus was dying we read, "So, when He heard that he was sick, He stayed two more days in the place where He was" (John 11:6). If we didn't know it was Jesus who purposely waited two days, we would have thought it was one of the disciples. Possibly it was Judas or Thomas who encouraged this delay. We may have thought that the responsible action of Jesus would have been to hurry to the house of Mary, Martha and Lazarus, and quickly perform the miracle. Again Jesus exemplifies rest. When we lift Him up and we see how great He is, and His love fills our hearts, we too will be at rest. This restful faith causes tumors to melt and slipped discs, hernias, joints and inflammations to be healed.

Jesus is relaxed in every situation. Consider the feeding of the five thousand. Even though Jesus knew what He was going to do, He asked Philip, "What do you think?" Jesus didn't say, "I am the Messiah. I have the revelation. You better start bringing some empty baskets or this miracle is not going to happen." No, Jesus is at rest.

You may have heard a lot of stressful preaching about how you must produce faith. It's one thing for healthy folks to be stressed out, but if you're on your deathbed and get taken into a healing service where they stress you out with so many instructions, it actually becomes worse than the hospital. That's not Jesus' ministry. For He said, "Come to Me, all you who labor and are heavy laden, and I will give you rest. Take My yoke upon you and learn from Me, for I am gentle and lowly in heart, and *you will find rest for your souls*. For My yoke is easy and My burden is light" (Matthew 11:28-30).

You need not be stressed about the size of your faith. Instead, allow Jesus to get bigger before your inward eyes. Is Jesus big enough to touch your family? To remove your tumor? Big enough for your lung problem, psoriasis, eczema, migraine? Is Jesus big enough to heal your cancer? How big is your Jesus?

Let nothing come between you and Jesus, not even your earnest attempt to have faith.

Before Jesus' death and resurrection, while still in the Old Covenant, Jesus frequently told people, "Your faith has made you whole." Never again were these words spoken once the New Covenant began after Jesus' death and resurrection. Never again are believers told, "Why don't you have faith?" You cannot be a born-again believer and be without faith. Once you are a believer, the author and finisher of faith lives inside of you.

These words "your faith has made you whole" were never spoken by the apostles Paul, John or Peter once Jesus had finished the work of His death and resurrection. Rather, Simon Peter looked at Aeneas who was lame, and said, "Jesus heals you." Philip went to Samaria and "preached Jesus Christ to them." Paul said, "I preach only 'Jesus Christ and Him crucified.'" The whole message and operation of miracles was centered on Jesus. The Holy Spirit glorifies Jesus. When we put the focus on Jesus, what He has done and His ability, the Holy Spirit works with us.

When you receive the healing you need while reading the pages of this book, please don't say, "Peter Youngren's ministry is really powerful." No, we don't want to exalt a ministry; we only want to lift up Jesus. I've heard too many statements like, "I have a ministry for back problems; I have a ministry for deaf ears; I have a ministry for stomach healings." It's about time we say, "I've got Jesus and He is all-sufficient." This way we don't have to seek healing or any specially anointed person, but our pursuit is after the Healer.

If nothing happens at first when we pray, then we just draw closer to Jesus and His Word.

We don't blame ourselves or others, but instead we ask the Holy Spirit for an ever clearer revelation of Jesus. The Book of Hebrews says, "For he who has entered His rest has himself also ceased from his works as God did from His" (Hebrews 4:10). Did you notice that? That rest comes when we cease from our own works. When we stop trying to have faith or earn our miracle, we can rest in Jesus' love and power.

NINE

Faith at the End of the Road

Faith flows freely when we are "nothing." When we are "nothing," Jesus is everything. The more "nothing" we are, the more faith will manifest.

Sometimes believers enjoy many repeated victories and blessings. Once we start serving the Lord, life gets better. Perhaps we are promoted at work, or our financial position improves; maybe we receive one or several wonderful answers to prayer. As time goes by we are tempted to feel invincible. That is why the Scripture encourages us, "Let him who thinks he stands, take heed lest he fall" (1 Corinthians 10:12). God doesn't want us to "fall," but sometimes it is only when people have experienced their own failure that the words of Jesus, "without Me you can do nothing," become a reality.

One of life's greatest discoveries is that without Jesus we are truly nothing. It is only "with God" that "all things are possible." The contrast is equally true; with man "it is impossible." When we rely on man's power and ability, the situation is hopeless. Good news! When our human hopelessness and nothingness are clear to us, we will find Jesus to be everything we need.

One common denominator between the Canaanite woman and the Roman centurion, those with "great faith," is that they were at the end of themselves.

This is exemplified repeatedly in the Bible. Elijah was filled with fear; he wanted to die because of the threatening words spoken by Queen Jezebel. At that low point he met God and walked for forty days in the strength of the divine encounter. Joshua sat with his face between his knees, a posture of discouragement, when he saw the "captain of the Lord's host." This divine encounter changed everything, and Joshua, with the people of Israel, marched around the walls of Jericho until they came down flat with the ground. Joseph was in the pit of despair in the dungeon of the prison, at the end of himself, when God exalted him to the palace in Egypt. Simon Peter had utterly failed by denying Jesus. In that state of despair, he encountered the Holy Spirit and preached and three thousand were saved. The patriarch Jacob demanded God's blessing, but it was not until he was wounded in his hip and limped that the blessings came. He had to come to the end of himself.

As long as we think or trust in ourselves as being good

enough Christians who live a better life than most, we will end up empty-handed. The truth is that we are all miserable failures without Jesus. Seeing our helplessness and hopelessness without Jesus sets the stage for Him to be our source, our everything.

Abraham experienced this truth. God had given him the promise that he would receive a son, but all along Abraham struggled with faith. Each time the Lord would visit him, Abraham would demonstrate his anguish of faith. He tried to convince God that Eleazar, his chief of staff, would be a suitable son of the promise. Later he and Sarah agreed that God's promise would be fulfilled through Abraham having a son with the maid Hagar. God loved and blessed Ishmael, who came through Abraham and Hagar's relationship, but God would not let him be the son of the promise.

Abraham's struggle continued for at least twenty-five years. Why couldn't Isaac have been born when Abraham was seventy-five years old and Sarah sixty-five? Could it be that they had to come to the end of themselves? They had to reach an age where a child was completely beyond all human reason? It had to be impossible? We read, "When Abram was ninety-nine years old, the LORD appeared to Abram and said to him, 'I am Almighty God (El Shaddai); walk before Me and be blameless'" (Genesis 17:1).

Abraham had tried to be "blameless." The people around him knew he was supposed to receive a son with Sarah, and it looked as if the promise would never be fulfilled. He sure looked like a fool. Abraham tried to make it happen in his own strength, but it only had an opposite effect.

God said, "I am El Shaddai." "El" means "God," and

"Shaddai" is translated "Almighty." The Hebrew word "shad" means "a woman's breast." Some have translated this, "I am the mother-breast-milk God." The picture of God is that of our sustainer or the One who nourishes, in the same way the milk from the mother's breast nourishes the newborn. God was saying, "Abraham, draw from Me all you need. I am your strength, your nourishment, your sustainer, your life giver; cling to Me." The message echoed strong in Abraham's heart, "You have tried in your own strength to be blameless and to make this miracle happen. Now instead just cling to El Shaddai, the Almighty. Rejoice in Him; let God be all that you need."

You will only find genuine faith in a close relationship with the Lord. No real faith exists outside of Jesus Himself. No matter how hard Abraham tried, fought, and struggled for the miracle to happen, he came up with nothing. He was to learn the lesson that each of us must learn: our only hope is in God. Jesus said, "Without Me you can do nothing," but when He is our life, nothing is impossible. Cling to Jesus, just like a baby clings to its mother. Let Jesus be your nourisher and sustainer.

Jesus saw a fig tree by the roadside. It had no figs, which was not surprising because it was not the season for figs. Jesus cursed the fig tree, and the next day when the disciples passed the same way, the fig tree was withered. They took note of it with astonishment.

Jesus used this event to teach the disciples to "have God's faith." We read, "So Jesus answered and said to them, 'Have faith in God'" (Mark 11:22). If you look at the literal translation it is, "Be you having faith of God," or "Have you faith of God." We could simply say:

Have the faith of God.

Jesus makes it clear to the disciples that in order to see this kind of wonder, it is not enough to have a mental believing; only God's faith will make it happen.

Then He explains how God's faith works. "For assuredly, I say to you, whoever says to this mountain, 'Be removed and be cast into the sea,' and does not doubt in his heart, but believes that those things he says will be done, he will have whatever he says. Therefore I say to you, whatever things you ask when you pray, believe that you receive them, and you will have them" (Mark 11:23-24).

When the faith of God is in operation there is no "doubt" in our hearts. We believe everything we say. This is not humanly possible. If you are hurting in your body, if the doctor has diagnosed you with a serious illness, you can tell your mind, "I believe, I believe." You can ask for prayer, but there is still a little tiny nagging question in your heart, "What if I am not healed?" That's human, and we have all experienced it. Jesus tells us of a faith where there is no doubt in your heart.

Many become disillusioned when they read Jesus' words, "Whatever things you ask when you pray believe that you have received them and you shall have them" (Mark 11:24). They write those words off, saying that it just doesn't work for them. It doesn't work if we try to make it happen through mental believing; it works only through God's faith.

Long before I ever understood these truths in Scripture, I saw them operating in real life situations. I was a very young preacher conducting a revival meeting in a little church in eastern Canada. A severely handicapped, retired Baptist lady was attending; I think she was intrigued by my message, but she was also very argumentative. She could only move about cautiously while leaning on her walker. After each service she would take me aside and ask questions about healing. I explained to her that it is God's will to heal, and she would argue this point. On another night I explained to her how Jesus bore every sickness and carried every pain on the cross, which is an awesome truth, but again she argued this and debated it from a theological position. One night the presence of Jesus swept over the meeting. The Baptist lady had hobbled to the front of the auditorium, her eyes wide open, leaning on her walker. Everyone was caught up in the presence of Jesus, worshiping Him. I forgot to keep my eye on the Baptist lady because I was also caught up with expressing my love toward Jesus. When I finally opened my eyes, I saw this lady at the back of the auditorium, praising and worshiping God with her arms in the air. This went on for some time until she suddenly opened her eyes, and a look of astonishment came over her face. I could tell that she was thinking, "Where is my walker?" As it turned out, her walker was still at the front of the auditorium. Now remember that for several years prior, she had not moved at all without this support. When the presence of Jesus filled the room, she forgot about her walker and moved to the back of the auditorium. She was healed while not even thinking about healing or seeking it, but just overwhelmed in the presence of Jesus.

She came for healing, but instead she met the Healer.

Do you see how her doubts vanished in the presence of Jesus? When His love and faith filled her heart, there was no further need for theological arguments. She believed without doubt and the miracle happened.

Ponder again the simple but liberating points I made earlier. These statements may be shocking and turn some of what you have heard previously upside down, yet these statements have brought liberty and freedom and opened the doors wide for Jesus' faith and healing power to flow:

1. *The faith of the sick and needy person is inadequate;*
2. *The faith of the one praying or preaching is inadequate;*
3. *The only adequate faith is Jesus' faith;*
4. *When Jesus' faith becomes our faith, we have mountain-moving faith;*
5. *Our task is to connect people with Jesus.*

You can connect with Jesus. He is ready to touch, lift and bless you. His presence is readily available wherever you are reading these words. Start to worship Him and thank Him right now. He is your El Shaddai. Call on Him; He will answer you.

The expression in Hebrews 12:2 is beautiful, "Looking unto Jesus, the author and finisher of faith." We don't look to Jesus, which would indicate that He is at some distance. Rather we are told to look unto Jesus. This indicates He is right here. We are like a baby looking unto its mother, drawing strength from the mother's breast. Jesus is our life, and when we pray, it is His life we receive. This is greater than a miracle; it is Jesus Himself, who is the source of every miracle, living in us.

PRAYER

"God, I come to You only trusting in what Jesus has done for me. Jesus, I believe You put my sins away by Your death on the cross. I believe You were wounded for my sins and that You bore my sickness and disease in Your body on the cross. Jesus, by Your stripes I have been healed. Thank You that You are the source of all I need. Holy Spirit, reveal Jesus more fully to me. Let Jesus become so great that any circumstance, situation or sickness will pale in comparison.

"Thank You, Jesus, for Your miracle life and power flowing through me. I promise to give all the praise only to You for all that You have done. Thank You, Jesus. Amen."

TEN

Obedience to the Faith

"Obey me because I said so" is an exasperated parent's final argument to a child unwilling to comply with what's requested. For many, our first encounter with the word obedience was when our parents tried to train us and we didn't want to go along. Maybe the word left a sour taste in our mouths. Perhaps you can relate to the story of the young boy who kept standing at the back of the classroom in spite of the teacher repeatedly telling him to sit down. Finally as the teacher starts to walk towards the back of the room the boy reluctantly sits down, but as soon as the teacher returns to the front of the classroom, he shouts, "I'm sitting on the outside, but I'm still standing on the inside."

According to the dictionary, obedience means *to do what someone tells you to do, to comply with or submit to authority; a rule or law*. This definition is typical of the world of religion with its many edicts and traditions that an adherent must follow. When the rules of any religion are challenged, the answer may be: don't ask questions, this is our faith, you better go along—obey!

The Greek word translated "obedience" in our Bibles is *hupakouo*. It contains three parts; *under — listen — comply*. We'll get back to that meaning and how it affects us in a moment, but first we look at the opposite—disobedience—which is at the root of sin. To disobey is to not come under, not listen and not comply.

We cannot understand obedience without looking at another unpopular word—*sin*. Within any religion there are usually lists of sins, which often vary depending on which part of the world you live in, your denominational affiliation and even your age. What's a sin in Argentina is not necessarily one in Siberia. What's acceptable conduct in an evangelical church in Europe may be considered sinful in the United States and vice versa. Your denominational affiliation may also have a huge bearing; Roman Catholics have their list of do's and don'ts, and so do Pentecostals, Charismatics, Baptists and Anglicans. Talk to your parents and you may discover that the definition of sin changes from generation to generation.

I grew up in a church environment where smoking cigarettes was considered a sign of a sinful life. If we saw someone smoke, surely this person could not be a Christian. I realize my memory could be clouded, but it seems we never paid as much attention to gossip, slander or pride. Our concept of sin had mostly to do with outward behavior, while the matters of the heart were ignored.

I realize now that I was robbed of a clear understanding. The narrow, legalistic definition of sin from my childhood was focused on a list of do's and don'ts, which was a smokescreen (no pun intended) to the real issue. Even sins like murder, adultery or stealing are but a byproduct of what sin really is.

One of the Scriptural definitions of sin is "missing the mark," or even better—"aiming at the wrong target." Adam, the first human, turned his attention from God, who is love, to a pursuit of self-discovery. Having his attention focused away from the mark—God's love—he was now compelled to try to invent a new reason for living.

Often sin is defined as a list of broken rules, but that only deals with the problem in a very superficial way. The root of sin is not broken rules but a broken relationship. Adam broke off relationship with God in the Garden of Eden. In Jesus's famous teaching in Luke chapter 15, the sheep broke off relationship with the shepherd, the coin was disconnected from the woman who treasured it, and the son walked away from a relationship with his father by going into a "far country."

The book of Romans describes sin as disobedience: "For as by one man's disobedience many were made sinners also by one man's obedience many will be made righteous" (Romans 5:19).

Remember the Greek word for obedience: under—listen—comply. Adam, the disobedient one, did not come under the love relationship with God that he was born to enjoy. Consequently he was unable to hear God's voice and, no longer knowing God's will, he was not able to do or comply with God's plan.

Sin is primal disobedience, a defiance of God's blueprint for living. It is a do-it-yourself plan. The essence of sin is to tell God to "take a hike," or "get out of my life."

One of the meanings of *Diablos*, the devil, is "the one who divides," a separator. Sin separates us from God and from others. We then separate people in categories of wealth, race or gender, and see ourselves as insiders or outsiders, depending on circumstances. Even worse, sin separates us from our self. We are forever on a quest to find ourselves. Often this results in a twisted sense of identity, because we no longer know who we are. That's why when you ask people who they are, they often respond by telling you what they do: I am a chef, a mechanic, a minister, a health worker, etc. Our sense of self has been reduced to a job or an educational award. Studies indicate that many people die shortly after retirement. Could it be that once the job is no longer there, the sense of identity is gone?

The tendency is to identify ourselves in terms of past events, positive or negative, be it an abusive relationship, a marriage breakup, a great reward we received, a great success or a great failure. Sometimes we define ourselves in terms of what others say about us, or worst of all, people define themselves by what their religion says about us.

In the case of definition of self through the lens of religion, it usually boils down to a list of tasks and performances, different suggestions of how the worshipers are supposed to please God. The will of God is presented as something to strive for, though difficult to find. People look at the will of God in terms of a geographical location; I don't know whether God has called me to stay in this city or to move on to another. In fact, the will of God is not about our geographical location, our employment or education, but it has everything to do with us getting back to the love relationship that we were born for. God's love is revealed through Jesus Christ, and we find our purpose through identification with Him. God's will is that you see yourself identified with Jesus Christ—He in us and us in Him.

Once we are separated from the love relationship we were created for, we will— knowingly or unknowingly— be on a quest to try to invent our identity and purpose of life.

The truth is that we are created in God's class. The first family—the Holy Trinity, Father, Son and Holy Spirit—existed in a mutual love relationship before the world was created. The purpose of creation was to invite us into that relationship of total love. Jesus called this pre-creation time the "bosom of the Father." It was a face-to-face, cheek-to-cheek relationship where the Father loved the Son and the Son loved the Father and the Holy Spirit celebrated that love. In this circle of love, God said, "Let Us make humans in our image." We were created to be included in this relationship where love is given, love is received, and love is celebrated.

Maybe this is a good time to go back and reread chapter 2, *Faith Works by Love.* God's love for you is unconditional, irreversible; there's no debate about it. God loves because He is love. When Adam and Eve sinned, God didn't turn into a raving vengeful maniac. He kept on loving. Forget all the grotesque misrepresentations of God, and look instead at Jesus Christ, who came to reintroduce God as God really is. He claimed that no one had seen the Father at any time, except the Son Jesus Christ (John: 1:18), a statement that disqualifies everyone else. The only accurate representation of God is Jesus Christ.

Our faith is rooted in who God is—LOVE— and what God did for the world—for you—through Jesus Christ. It is this faith that we are called to obey.

Obey the faith! Obey the representation of God shown to us by Jesus Christ! Obey the reality that God unconditionally loves you! Stop fighting it, arguing against it—*accept your acceptance.*

Jesus is our example of obedience:

He humbled himself and became obedient to the point of death, even the death of the cross. (Philippians 2:8)

Jesus did the opposite of Adam. He submitted Himself under His Father's love, listened to His Father and only did what He heard and saw His Father do. Jesus complied with the Father's will, not only to death, but to the death of cross.

Roman citizens could not be crucified. It was considered too sadistic, torturous, sub-human. The biblical narrative tells us that "wicked people," who represented all wicked people throughout all time, came at Jesus. It was as if they attacked Him with their teeth bared, their claws out, viciously beating Him until He was unrecognizable. Jesus became totally identified with every form of wickedness known to humanity. The first Adam had brought death (separation from God) into creation, and now Jesus Christ absorbed the shame and guilt of every disobedience and evil. He experienced the bitterness of human deception, betrayed with a kiss, not with a slap.

The cross is the description of God entering inside human suffering at its worst. Jesus was disfigured and humiliated. The perverts laughed as he hung naked on the cross. History repeated itself as the multitude cried out, "Away with him, crucify him." It wasn't the street people, the prostitutes, the thieves or the professional swindlers, known as tax collectors, who crucified Jesus.

Religious people killed Jesus Christ.

Religion has never accepted this God of love, who Jesus represented, but instead prefers a mean, vindictive, petty and angry deity.

Some may interject that my teaching here is one-sided. They will correctly state that Jesus mentioned hell, judgment and showed anger. Yes He did, but it was always directed at the same people—the religious leaders who tried to block the way of grace for common people. There's not one case of Jesus angrily denouncing thieves, prostitutes or tax collectors. Yes, Jesus spoke of hell more than anyone else, and His comments were always directed at the religious elite.

God had always been willing and able to forgive, and the ultimate evidence of this is seen at the cross and resurrection of Jesus. This was God in Jesus Christ reconciling the whole world to Himself (2 Corinthians 5:19). The wicked hands put on Jesus imparted every evil known to humankind onto Him. He identified with the worst wickedness known, defeated it and rose again to offer new life to everyone.

The difference between the first Adam (Jesus Christ) and the last Adam is found in this one word—obedience. One early church teacher wrote that when Satan came at Jesus, he bit off more than he could chew. Satan had easily chewed on Adam, the disobedient one, but he couldn't chew Jesus Christ, the obedient one.

Jesus was the first human to refuse Satan's lies. We are so accustomed to thinking of Jesus as the Son of God that we easily forget that Jesus was the Son of Man, fully human. He had laid aside all the use of His divine attributes to become one of us. Jesus became hungry, tired, sad and in need of encouragement, physically, mentally and emotionally, in every way as us.

Jesus was the first human who obeyed God's love plan.

Satan tempted Jesus to jump off the pinnacle of the temple or to command stones to become bread, and he prefaced those temptations by saying, "If you are the son of God." In principle there was nothing wrong with jumping off the pinnacle of the temple or commanding stones to become bread. But that wasn't the issue. The real issue for Satan was to get Jesus to doubt who He was. Satan was in essence telling Jesus, "Maybe you are not the one in whom the Father is well pleased, maybe you're not the one you think you are."

Satan attacked Jesus in the same way that he attacks us, by causing us to doubt who we are. His attacks on you may sound like this: "How can God love you after everything you've done? You should have done better, God expected more of you; look at how you've let others and yourself down," and on and on it goes.

Jesus didn't fall for Satan's lies. He obeyed the love plan.

Some people have erroneously suggested that the teaching of God's love and grace is just a sweet message to encourage people. It's much more than that. It is a life-transforming reality that goes against every religious instinct. It is a message that says you are unconditionally loved and accepted by God.

God loves you irreversibly. He proved it by sending Jesus Christ to identify with humanity at its worst, defeat evil and triumphantly rise from the dead, in order to provide new life for everyone.

That's our faith.

Believe it.

Obey it!

You are included in Jesus Christ, in His death, resurrection and in His exalted state at the right hand of the Father.

John said, "As He is so are we in this world" (1 John 4:17).

Come under God's love plan!

Jesus Christ was wounded for our transgressions and bruised for our iniquities and by his stripes we were healed (1 Peter 2:21). Obey that!

The first century church was on a mission to get the world to obey the faith of the Gospel. Paul, the apostle, said that God gave him "grace...for <u>obedience to the faith</u>" (Romans 1:5). He told the Corinthian believers to bring "every thought into captivity to the <u>obedience of Christ</u>" (2 Corinthians 10:5).

Contrary voices and disobedient thoughts arise in our minds to contradict the revelation of God that Jesus gave us. These voices bombard our thinking and imagination to tell us that we are not loved by God, that we're not valuable, that life is in vain, that God has given up on us. It seems these negative thoughts hit us the hardest when we suffer sickness or some other difficulty. This is the time people question, "Why me, why not someone else? It must have been something I did wrong." Take those thoughts of disobedience and put them into captivity under Jesus Christ's finished work.

Paul seemed frustrated when he wrote to the Galatian believers. They had a good start in the Christian faith, but after a while religious legalism had twisted their understanding of the Gospel, not unlike what we see sometimes today. He wrote, "Who hindered you from obeying the truth?" (Galatians 5:17). It wasn't a mere nuance of doctrine; they had stopped obeying the truth of the finished work of Jesus Christ.

Again in describing his mission, the apostle said that he was called to "make the Gentiles obedient" (Romans 15:18).

Obedience is the key.

Obey the reality that you are loved, that Christ took your sin, guilt and shame, and put it away forever.

Someone may question, "How do we know that the call to obedience was not a call to obey religious rules, ceremonies or commandments?" Look at every context of the Scriptures we have quoted, and you will discover that the writers are not talking about obedience to any religious institution, dogma or ceremony, but to the revelation of Jesus Christ.

One telling Scripture is found in Acts 6:7, "a great many of the priests were obedient to the faith...."

This is a reference to the priests within the Jewish religion. We can assume that they were already following the Ten Commandments to the best of their ability. They kept the Hebrew feasts and complied with the ceremonial rules. By the standard of religion we would have to conclude that they were obedient, but their obedience was to a religion, not to the faith of the Gospel. After hearing the Gospel, they who had obeyed performances and ceremonies became obedient to the revelation of God through Jesus Christ.

Sadly, still today, 2000 years after the revelation of the finished work of Jesus, many speak of obedience only in terms of religious rules, traditions and edicts. True obedience, according to the New Testament, is to obey what Christ has done for us, and who He has shown that God is.

Look at the three parts of the Greek word *hupakouo* again:

Under: This is not to live under rules and ceremonies but to live under God's love plan. You are God's beloved, loved by the Heavenly Father with the same quality of love that Jesus enjoyed. You are a joint heir with Christ.

Listen/Hear: We can only accurately hear from God after we recognize His love. As long as we live in a performance-based religion, we will think that we hear God calling us to ever new performances. We will be on that treadmill of self-effort that gets us nowhere.

Comply: Once we obey that we are loved and identified with Christ, we can hear God's voice, and once we hear it we are able to do His will.

See it! Believe it! Obey it!

I said earlier that faith is not difficult. On the contrary, real faith is as natural as the blood flowing through your veins. Go back over the truths I have shared in this book again and again. Why this continued focus? Because an academic knowledge of God's love is not enough; it must be known experientially, because this is a love which passes academic and mental knowledge. You will grow in faith by seeing the width, height, length and depth of Christ love. How does it happen?

I suggest three landmarks on our journey to ever-increasing faith:

Cognitive understanding: This is where we see the truth of God's grace and love factually. Our mental understanding is open to the fact that the Gospel is greater than we thought it was. We understand that God's love is far greater than any human love; it's a different kind of love altogether. We understand that Jesus Christ bore our sins and carried our sicknesses, that everything from God is available to us by grace alone, without any merits of our own. Still, our journey must go beyond cognitive understanding.

Emotional mastery: This is where our feelings, imagination and emotions are involved. We go over the same truths again and again, and as we do, our senses are stimulated. We think, talk and dream of God's love for us and for others. Our faith is nurtured. It is growing day by day, but there's still more.

The intuitive faith life: This is where we live by the faith of Jesus Christ. "As a person thinks in his heart so is he," is a saying repeated several times in the Book of Proverbs. Stay focused on God's love and faith will grow ever stronger. The intuitive faith life is where you are free from legalistic, self-loathing, self-condemning thoughts, and instead you live in the light of God's love.

That's the love zone. That's the faith zone. The two are interconnected. You no longer try to produce faith, but instead you live in the assurance of God's unconditional, irreversible love for you.

That's where the real faith is, because "faith works by love" (Galatians 5:6).

That's the only faith that works. That's the faith that causes you to speak to your mountain to move. Faith without limits—rooted in the revelation of Jesus Christ.

Connect with Peter

UNITED STATES
P.O. Box 2108, Vista, CA 92085-2108
PH. 1 760-751-3374

CANADA
190 Railside Rd, Toronto, ON M3A 1A3
PH. 1 416-497-4940

For product orders, call 1-877-974-7223

 E-mail: info@peteryoungren.org

 Website: www.peteryoungren.org

 Twitter: @peteryoungren

 Facebook: peterjyoungren

 YouTube: celebratingjesus

Friendship Festivals: Friendship Festivals are Gospel campaigns held throughout the world, with a strong focus on nations and people groups that are "unreached". Crowds of 50,000 to 600,000 people regularly gather in a single service.

Pastors' & Leaders' Seminar: Seminars for pastors and church leaders run concurrent with each Friendship Festival. The focus is on training pastors and leaders to advance the Gospel in their own region. More then 350,000 pastors have been trained.

Television & Media: "You Are Loved" is seen daily on television and internet web sites throughout the world. Now partnering in Pakistan for 24/7 Gospel TV in the world's largest Muslim city.

Follow Up for New Believers: "Salvation - God's Gift to You" has been distributed to over 16 million new believers in multiple languages.

Bible School: World Impact Bible Institute was established in 1988. To date, more than 3,300 students from over 30 nations have been trained to advance the Gospel. Campuses are located in North America, East Africa, and Asia.

Literature & Resource Distribution: Peter Youngren is the author of over 20 books and study manuals that have been translated into numerous languages.

Long-Term Missions: Missionaries have been sent to Kenya, Indonesia, Gambia, Thailand, Papua New Guinea, Ethiopia, Croatia, Democratic Republic of Congo, Philippines and Guatemala.

Ministry in Israel - Way of Peace: This ministry operates in Israel daily, by empowering local evangelists and pastors to share the message of Jesus Christ with their local communities.

Ministry to political/business leaders: The focus is to share the Gospel with political, business, and religious leaders. This often opens doors that have long been closed to the Gospel.

Prayer Center: Prayer is an integral part of every ministry aspect. Thousands of prayer requests are received weekly via the phone, mail and email from every continent.

The Grace Manifesto (8cd)
This verse by verse study through the book of Galatians will leave an indelible mark on your spiritual life. The apostle is more "in our face" in his writings to the Galatians than any other time. Truly a revolutionary teaching that answers the questions that many have.
$64.00

The Love That Won't Let Go (6cd)
Luke chapter 15 is one of the most beloved teachings of Jesus, where he addresses the religious leaders of his day. A life transforming revelation of God's love.
$48.00

Hesed: Discover Your Covenant of Loving Kindness (4cd)
An incredible revelation of the Agape love of God.
$32.00

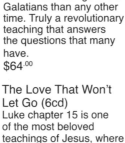

Faith (7cd)
What it is! What it looks like! How it really works. Do you feel that you need more faith? Discover how Jesus' own faith can be yours.
$56.00

Freedom From Sin Consciousness (3c)
Sin-consciousness w stunt your spiritual a personal developme set free into the reali Christ consciousness
$24.00

Can You See Wha God Sees... For Y (6cd)
Through Scrip and practical examp Peter reveals how G sees you, and how c is transformed by se what God sees.
$48.00

The Amazing Tru About You! (4cd)
Get to know yourse better and you will others and the wor around you in a ne light.
$32.00

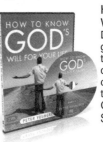

How to Know Go Will for your Life
Discover the three given by God to al take us in the right direction. A teachin designed to help y through life confide God's purpose for
$16.00

More resources available online at:

www.peteryoungren.org/store

Grace
Prayer Center

Let us pray with you in the

light of Christ's finished work

CALL WITH YOUR PRAYER REQUESTS
OR PRAISE REPORTS

1.877.974.7223

SUBMIT ONLINE 24/7

peteryoungren.org/prayer